Praise for Janna Hoiberg and *The Family Business*

"*Successful family enterprises require careful attention to best practices. Janna Hoiberg's business experience, insights and accomplished perspective bring practical focus to what makes family-owned businesses work and thrive in* The Family Business. *This book is a must read for anyone wanting to achieve sustainable results and profitable outcomes.*"

—KEVIN KNEBL, International Speaker/Author/Trainer/Advisor

"*Janna is really great at working with family owned businesses. As a business coach, Janna is able to relate to both men and women family business owners. She has often helped me to find a balance between running an ever-more successful business and being able to focus on my family, so that I can also fulfill my lifelong dream of being a wonderful mom and a successful family owned business.*"

—HEATHER LANGTON, President, TLC Design/Build Remodeling

"*Awesome book, really tells it like it is and provides a path for improving the family owned business. This is a must read for anyone in a family business.*"

—CHRIS REYNOLDS, Platinum Relations

"*Janna's immense business acumen combined with her fun spirit make her a tremendously effective coach.*"

—CHRIS BURGHARDT, Owner, Jazy Frei Plumbing and Heating, Inc.

"*The key principles clarity, focus, and execution are pivotal to my own success acceleration approach, taught and used by premier corporations around the globe. In order to get to the best results faster, this is especially true for local and family owned business enterprises. Janna Hoiberg makes these principles come alive in* The Family Business. *Best practices, case studies, and insights from her accomplished experience make this book a must read for any business owner, new or established.*"

—TONY JEARY, The RESULTS Guy™

The FAMILY BUSINESS

How to Be in Business with People You Love

. . .Without Hating Them

JANNA HOIBERG

The Family Business: How to Be in Business with People You Love . . .
Without Hating Them

Copyright © 2013, Janna Hoiberg

Published by
Harvest Enterprises Press
620 North Tejon Street, Suite #101
Colorado Springs, CO 80903
www.jannahoiberg.com

ISBN: 978-1-940342-00-9

Cover and Interior Design: Desktop Miracles, Inc.

Publisher's Cataloging-In-Publication Data
(*Prepared by The Donohue Group, Inc.*)

Hoiberg, Janna.
    The family business : how to be in business with people you love—without hating them / Janna Hoiberg.
        p. : ill. ; cm.
    Issued also as an ebook.
    Includes bibliographical references.
    ISBN: 978-1-940342-00-9
1. Family-owned business enterprises.   2. Work and family.   3. Interpersonal communication   4. Success in business.   I. Title.

HD62.25 .H65   2013

                                                    658.04

Printed in the United States of America

"For I know the plans I have for you,"
declares the Lord,
"plans to prosper you and not to harm you,
plans to give you hope and a future."
JEREMIAH 29:11

Dedication

Aheartfelt thank you goes to my friends, previous employers, business owners, clients and family for all your support in writing this book. I appreciate all of you for the stories, experiences and feedback you have provided. Thank you to my coaches and advisory board for candid feedback on all parts of my life to help me grow and get this accomplished.

I dedicate this book to every family owner. My wish is that you apply even one concept to your business and make a difference. I dedicate this as well to Steve and Andrew—for allowing stories about them and to God who loves me no matter what I do for His plan to prosper me in ways I cannot even begin to imagine.

—JANNA

"Changing the way you think about business."

Contents

Preface   11
Introduction   17

PART ONE

DEFINING A FAMILY BUSINESS

CHAPTER 1   Why Do We Have Family Businesses?   25
CHAPTER 2   Foundations for a Successful Family Business   33
CHAPTER 3   The Upside of the Family Business   61
CHAPTER 4   The Downside of the Family Business   67
CHAPTER 5   Finding the Balance Between Work and Play   77

PART TWO

MOTIVATION FOR HAVING A FAMILY BUSINESS

CHAPTER 6   Mindset   87
CHAPTER 7   Control   91
CHAPTER 8   Passion for a Product or Service   101
CHAPTER 9   Buying a Job   107
CHAPTER 10   Career Change   111
CHAPTER 11   Turning a Hobby into a Business   125

PART THREE

RELATIONSHIPS IN A FAMILY BUSINESS

CHAPTER 12   How do I Fire My Wife (or Husband)?   131
CHAPTER 13   Communication   163
CHAPTER 14   Boundaries   177

PART FOUR

EVOLUTION OF A FAMILY BUSINESS

CHAPTER 15   Wills and Estate Planning   185

CHAPTER 16   Creating the Legacy   201

CHAPTER 17   Passing the Torch   207

Conclusion   215
Books to Read   217

Preface

Family is the cornerstone of society. A family provides love, support, friendship, acceptance and companionship. Family can also be the cornerstone of conflict, frustration, disappointment and rejection. Family businesses mirror the family. They provide support, friendship, acceptance and economic support. The family business can also manifest itself in disappointment, divisiveness, frustration and anger. The challenge is how to ensure the family business becomes or remains positive and does not become a source of negativity.

The strengths of family ties are often seen in the family business environment. A local business in town is comprised of parents, four children working in the business, and probably 30 additional employees. Each family member had a role in the business and supported each other both at work and outside the office. They worked together, played together and remained a cohesive unit. Yes, there were times they fought at work; they had learned to fight as siblings. They also learned to not take it personally (at least not long term). I heard the same response from the family members many times: "I would never be in this business if it weren't the family business. I love it, have learned a great deal, it has supported our family for over 25 years but would never recommend it to another family." The toils are great, the rewards are great and they see their own children continuing in the business, but caution others considering the journey.

Families are at the heart of society. Statistics indicate there are more than 16 million small businesses in the U.S. alone. Small businesses range from home-based environments to structured operational business environments with employees and millions of dollars in revenue. Family businesses make up 80 percent of small businesses in the U.S. Working for a family business when you are not family can have great rewards as well as great challenges.

> *Most owners of family businesses don't realize the impact the business has on their family and the employees.*

This book focuses on the joys, challenges, opportunities and threats encountered in the family business—to the family, the employees and the future of the business. Additionally, this book discusses the relationships of family members to other family members, employees and the outside world, i.e., customers, as well as working in a multigenerational environment.

If you are considering starting a family business, continue reading. This book will open your eyes to the joys and challenges and help you structure your business so it is of greater value to your family and your community. You may not have considered many of the topics discussed here, such as the consuming nature of the business, the challenge it poses to relationships, the impact of failure and the impact of success.

If you are already running a family business, read on. Most owners of family businesses don't realize the impact the business has on their family and the employees. They see the business as an extension of themselves, which can be hard on other family members and employees. Having a family member decide to leave the business or not join can be devastating; if you are saying "that won't happen to us," then think again.

If you are employed by a family business, you are living the joys and challenges. The sense of family is both the good and the challenging part of your job. You love being in the family environment, yet some family members get away with things that you would be fired for doing in another organization. The ability to be promoted and rise in the company may be severely limited.

If you know someone who owns a family business and wonder whether all family businesses are the same, read on. You might learn a few things and be able to understand where they are and what they are going through. You might even pass along this book; it will make a difference in their business and in their personal lives.

This book is geared toward the small business owner. "Small" is a relative term. For purposes of this book, small is defined as under $30 million in revenue. It doesn't mean the premise is different for the larger company; however, there are other books focused on larger entities. The goal here is to give the small family business owner the tools to grow into that large family business without having the family unit hold them back and to provide a firm foundation for the family business to grow and be able to give back to the family, their employees and society.

> *The resulting joy, hardship, challenge, growth and opportunity are dependent on how well you manage those relationships.*

The book is divided into four parts. The first provides the foundation and definitions of the small family business (which really isn't different from any small business). It looks at the aspects that any family business must consider, whether it is just starting out or has been around for decades.

The second part is geared toward the family that is considering starting a family business. It discusses the motivations and common reasons that people start a business.

Part Three applies to all family businesses and focuses on what is at the core of the challenges—relationships. You can pick your friends, but you can't pick your relatives (other than your spouse). The resulting joy, hardship, challenge, growth and opportunity are dependent on how well you manage those relationships.

Part Four challenges you to consider the legacy you want to leave and discusses moving the business from one generation to another or to an owner outside the family.

In all things a foundation must be laid. In writing this book, I used a number of biblical principles. These principles apply in all aspects of life and society. It is not meant to preach, yet being a Christian myself, these principles are at the core of who I am and how I have run businesses for over 30 years. You can take them as stories and apply them in your own way and through your own spiritual lens. No matter what your faith, the Bible is also a book of history and provides great lessons on how the family business has been around for centuries. We can all learn from history.

The research in the book is based on years of up close and practical experience. While there is more formal research on family businesses, most of the stories presented here are taken from years of running and coaching businesses. This involves eight businesses in more than 40 years of being an employee, a stockholder, and a business owner. As a coach I have coached over 100 businesses, spoken with another 100 about their business and interviewed another 50 specifically for this book. It is that real-life experience that is presented in these pages.

My journey in life has taken me through a number of family businesses starting with my dad and being involved in a family business growing up—the family farm. Grandpa was the business owner, Dad and his five brothers were the employees and Grandma ran the business from the house. Grandpa may have run the outside day-to-day business, but trust me, Grandma ran the business. Employees were hired during the busy season and they moved on during the slow season. Work needed to be done, crops needed to be harvested, bills needed to be paid and the future needed to be secured. It was a family business in all ways. Much was learned from that family business. Two of the brothers continued in the tradition, yet in what has become common, it didn't make it past the second generation. The brothers chose to sell that family business, with one retiring and the other moving to a different job. The third generation wanted no part of it.

Dad moved away from the farm and took a job as an employee—a salesperson to be exact. Yet when the opportunity came, he took advantage of all he had learned in the family business and became a business owner once again. It started small—repairing lawn mower engines (and go-carts, which were a lot of fun). That led to buying an apartment complex—all while still working as an employee. Then he hit the wall at his sales job. He was informed that there was no more advancement for him. Nothing further, no challenges; just the same thing day after day, week after week, year after year.

That entrepreneurial spirit rose up, and he and my mom (notice the family business concept again) purchased a mobile home park about an hour away from where we lived in California. With $1,000 in their bank account (it was the 1970s), Dad quit his job and my parents made this new business their livelihood. It became the past, present and future. Everything they had rode on this venture and its success. They moved into a mobile home in the park. (Another common theme—the family business and life commingle.) They purchased it with friends who were partners. Now they had not only a family business but two families as partners in a family business. If

We often cannot change what we don't see.

there was something more dangerous, I am not sure what it was, other than the bear that lived in the gold mine (no gold) at the bottom of the hill next to the sewer pond (the same sewer pond that Dad fell into while on a small rowboat trying to fix a problem in the pond). All of this was a part of everyday life for me growing up.

At age 20 I moved to Boston and essentially spent a good portion of the next 30 years working in and with family-owned businesses. Sometimes it was the customers who were the family-owned business, sometimes it was my employer, sometimes it was the vendors. Through it all I gained respect, appreciation, experience and stories that are shared in this book.

Not all the stories have happy endings. Not all family businesses have a fairy-tale existence. The purpose of this book is to help family members in a business better understand the impact the business has on the family, and the effects their behavior has on the business so they may modify their behavior where necessary or desired. Another purpose of this book is to better prepare the individual who is considering starting or purchasing a family-owned business. We often cannot change what we don't see. If we don't understand the effects the business has on our lives, then we cannot use the strengths and weaknesses of the environment to make the necessary changes.

Use this book as an educational tool, a resource and a way to make your family business the best in your community.

As a note: The names and some of the details in this book have been changed to protect the privacy of those involved. However, they are all real-life stories of businesses, people, experiences and results achieved.

Introduction

Two brothers, Jay and Ron, married best friends from childhood; they loved their families and each other, and were passionate about fixing up cars. One day they decided to buy a body shop and work for themselves. Their parents were so excited to see their sons embrace the American dream that they invested a great deal of their savings to bankroll this endeavor. The brothers, confident in their plan, put their homes up as collateral for the business loan.

After checking out numerous body shops they finally found the perfect one that fit their needs. There was, however, one missing ingredient—someone with a business background. The brothers invited a childhood friend, Joe, to join them to take care of the books and provide input regarding business decisions. Business was good and they were able to hire a couple of guys to help out. Everything was going according to plan, and on the one-year anniversary of the brothers' business the whole family got together at a nice restaurant and had dinner, complete with cake, to celebrate their success. That's the last pleasant memory anyone has.

At the beginning of the second year, Joe got married and moved about 50 miles away with his new bride. He was content to manage things from afar and trusted Ron and Jay to take care of the daily business transactions. The brothers thought this was a good plan. Unfortunately, while they still loved the work, they had no idea how much time needed to be devoted to paying bills and keeping things afloat on the business side of the house. This was the beginning of the end; their American dream became their American nightmare.

No one questioned what was going on because the brothers always said that things were going well. They began to work extremely long hours because now they were doing not only their work but Joe's as well. The long days turned into weeks, which turned into months. The hours and pressure began to build.

There seemed to be endless requests for more money to be put into the business. The parents, once so eager to invest, were tapped out, and no one could remember the last time the brothers took a paycheck. They began to withdraw money from their personal bank accounts to cover the bills, many times without their wives knowing—that is, until their personal checks started to bounce! Jay even took the money his children inherited from their great-grandmother in an effort to stop the hemorrhage, but the business kept bleeding out.

The pressure became unbearable and Ron started using drugs to manage both the long hours and the stress. He also added to the business's problems by taking the employee withholding tax money to fund his habit. With Joe out of the picture, and Jay interested only in fixing cars, Ron was able to sustain this lifestyle for quite a while.

No one can quite remember when the first domino fell, but things unraveled quickly. The IRS and many other creditors wanted their money, there was no cash to pay the substantial outstanding debts, the brothers' home life was strained to the breaking point, and the family was at odds. To compound matters, the issues with the IRS were actual crimes, and the brothers faced possible jail time. Finally Jay and his wife decided they needed to act quickly to put an end to the string of bad decisions that were all aimed at hiding the reality of the problem. They chose bankruptcy, which meant they defaulted on the business loan and the business folded—as did their relationship with Ron and his family.

They lost their house of 13 years, and their children were uprooted from the only home they'd ever known. They moved in with Jay's wife's parents in a neighboring state. That was over 20 years ago!

There was a lot of collateral damage from the falling house of cards. When Ron and Jay parted company, it left their parents in the middle, their wives (who had been best friends for more than three decades by this point) at odds, and the cousins (their children) suddenly separated from each other. More than 13 years elapsed before there would be an intentional meeting, a week spent together in Florida for their parents' 50th wedding anniversary celebration.

For Ron's kids there was a great deal of confusion. Because they were young when the business died, they didn't have strong memories of their Uncle Jay or aunt or cousins. It was a bittersweet week, especially for Jay's wife and oldest daughter, both of whom had fond memories of their time with Ron's oldest son, Mason. He was interested in why he didn't really know this part of his family existed, especially since his mother and aunt had been such close friends. His aunt spent hours recounting childhood tales of his mother as well as precious memories of her time spent with him. Mason asked what her favorite memory was of him and she said, "Driving you home from vacation Bible school while you taught me the Barney song." All of a sudden, she saw the spark of recognition in his eyes and they softly sang the song together all those years later. Ron and Jay's dad was often teary-eyed that week as he reveled in the reuniting of his once-close family that had been torn apart by a family business gone bad.

This same family would be reunited three months later when Ron and Jay's father passed away unexpectedly. Over the past few years there have been moments when the family has all been together, but they are few and far between and hinge on visits from their mom. There are still many family milestones celebrated without the aunt, uncle, or cousins. Their greatest fear is that once their mom passes there will be no more moments. Damage that deep is never truly repaired. If only there was someone who could have counseled them on how to start a family business without ruining the family, their lives would look radically different today.

The above is a true story.

Let's look at another family business:

Back in 1927, George Perkins began his career operating garages on the Western Slope of Colorado. In 1941 he moved to Colorado Springs, where he operated service stations around the Colorado Springs area. In 1945 he opened the DeSoto Plymouth franchise that is today Perkins Motors.

What George didn't know when he started his business was that his legacy would span four generations of business owners and would become and remain a very successful business. George died unexpectedly in 1959 and Will Perkins took over as president. Tom Perkins started working in the family business in 1973, became president in 1985 and has since transitioned the role of president to his son David.

There is a family bond that transcends the generations. They have worked together and played together. The kids spent years working in the business, from weeding spare lots to driving vehicles from one part of the business to another. As the family grew, not everyone chose to remain in the family business; some went off to follow other passions. Fortunately, each generation produced one family member who remained passionate about the business. It has been a hard 80-plus years. Business has been good; business has been bad. Suppliers have come and gone, the industry has changed, and the family has grown.

The constant has been the business and the legacy it has generated. Very seldom do you find a four-generation family business that works, is profitable and has created a lasting legacy. Forty-three percent of family-owned businesses will transition from the first generation to the second generation; 30 percent will survive the second generation; 15 percent will successfully pass to the third generation; and only 3 percent will make it to the fourth generation, according to the Institute for Family-Owned Business. The family's legacy transcends the business. The business focus is to give back to the community and to Christian organizations. Will, Tom and David all attribute their family values and focus to their personal relationship with God. They have succeeded in many ways: community impact, employer, mission to serve others. It is a family that loves to work together and play together, even vacationing as an extended family.

Is life always perfect? Of course not; life isn't perfect. They have struggled, disagreed, and fought, but found a common bond in family that tied them together through thick and thin.

This is the success story and one that should happen far more.

Answering the question "What could have been done to prevent the first story from happening?" is the cornerstone of this book. Business owners face many challenges and many opportunities.

PART ONE

Defining a Family Business

The family business has been around for centuries. They have evolved, grown, and been the foundation of civilization. There is a tremendous upside to the family business, full of joy and opportunity. There is also a downside filled with lost opportunity and division. Creating a strong foundation and maintaining that foundation will benefit the business in the years to come and is worth the time and effort to create.

CHAPTER 1

Why Do We Have Family Businesses?

Tim loved to be in control. He really didn't like others telling him what to do and was always thinking of better ways to run a business than his current employer. He was tired of the poor compensation for the work he put in, especially when he compared himself to other employees. Tim had an idea.

Fortunately, Tim was married to Tina. Where Tim was all over the board with new ideas, Tina was organized, loved to spend time with people and was energized by Tim's new ideas. Tim's new idea was for them to go into business for themselves. After all, they got along well and were of the same mindset in many areas. They had saved up some money while working for others, so why not start their own business. They had both been in the business world in their respective careers for a number of years, so they knew what needed to be done to make a business successful. Also, Tim's brother, Alan, had some of the same skill sets as Tim and was bored of his current job. Maybe once they got the business started they could bring in Alan to help as well. The excitement was building.

The above scenario (or one like it) is played out countless times over kitchen tables all around the world when people begin to think about the possibilities of the family business.

There are many drivers for starting a family business, including the following passions:

- Desire for control—I don't want to work for someone else.
- Hobby turned into a business—This hobby could make money.
- Second career—I could retire from my first career (or second) and start another one.
- Passion for a product/idea—This will save the world, the community, my family.
- Buying a job—I can't find work, but I'm ready to contribute to society.
- Skill in an area—I want to share this skill I have with others and get paid for it.
- Serial entrepreneurs—The first time was fun; let's do it again and again and again.

Several of these passions often combine to drive the start of the business. The eventual success of the business usually depends on how well the new business owners transition from startup mentality (I have to/must do everything myself) to the business owner mentality which means I must look at what is right for the business. This means doing things like: plan, delegate, grow, invest, step back etc.

What Really Is a Family Business?

The family business defined: "In a family business, two or more members within the management team are drawn from the owning family. Family businesses can have owners who are not family members. Family businesses may also be managed by individuals who are not members of the family. However, family members are often involved in the operations of their family business in some capacity and, in smaller companies, usually one or more family members are the senior officers and managers. (Wikipedia 12/30/11)

> *When you start looking at the business through the eyes of the business owner, your perspective will change.*

Family participation as managers and/or owners of a business can strengthen the company because family members are often loyal and dedicated to the family enterprise. However, family participation as managers and/or owners of a business can present unique problems because the dynamics of the family system and the dynamics of the business systems are often not in balance.

Let's say you own a painting business. What are you first—the painter or the business owner?

How do you think most painters who are business owners respond?

Now apply this to your business. What are you first—the skilled provider of the product or service or the business owner?

What is your answer? If the answer to the hypothetical is "painter," then you need to step back. As long as you continue to be a painter first and business owner second, you will look at the business through the eyes of a painter. When you start looking at the business through the eyes of the business owner, your perspective will change. You will read your financial statements and will understand profitability. You will look at what is true customer service (and don't say yours is great; everyone says that) and will determine what is WOW customer service. WOW Customer Service is the service you get from a business that makes you step back and say WOW. To keep your customers today, you can't be content just to satisfy them. If you want your business to thrive you have to create what Ken Blanchard calls "Raving Fans". These are customers who are so excited about the way you treat them that they want to tell everyone about you. Zappos, the on-line shoe store has put Deliver

WOW in Service as one of their foundational culture statements for the business. You will understand and manage your sales funnel to increase your business. You will manage your team with the thought of growth, teamwork and reducing turnover.

The business owner should also look to the strength of each family member. This will allow them to step out of the family role and into the business owner role. The sooner that transition takes place, the faster the business as an enterprise will begin to grow. Surveys have shown that many successful family business owners, if they had to do it all over, would take much of the "family" emotion and control out of the business environment sooner. It is harder to take out the "family" emotion after the business is growing and on a roll than it is to lay the groundwork from the beginning. The business would have grown stronger and faster and the returns greater. Now this doesn't mean it is all business and no pleasure. However, cutting family drama to a minimum goes a long way toward profitability.

How is that a different perspective from the painter who just wants to paint the wall? This doesn't change the fact that the owner/tradesman needs to paint the wall and do a fantastic job delivering the product and service. It does change what they do with their non-billable hours. It also changes their understanding of how to leverage their time to build the business rather than being *in* the business 50 hours per week 52 weeks per year.

Value: Each business must provide value. Each business owner must determine the value of what they provide to their customers. The word value has about six meanings depending on how the word is used. Value of:

- Education
- Goods or services
- Money
- Music
- Number
- Principals

When it comes to value in the business, here are some questions to answer:

+ What is value to you?
+ How do you value your business?
+ How do you create value in the family business and what is the value you want to create?
+ How does that value equate to the goals of the family?
+ What value are your creating in the community?

Very few business owners ever define what value they really want to create in their business, nor do they truly attempt to create a valuable business that will sustain itself. While this is true to some extent in all businesses, I find it even more the case in the family business.

Value is in the eyes of the beholder, but let's consider two scenarios. Two businesses start at the same time, essentially in the same market serving the same types of customers. Both are family-owned businesses with the husband and wife in the business. One approaches the business as essentially a job. He talks about creating value, but the business and the family live paycheck to paycheck. When business picks up, the marketing decreases, which causes subsequent quarters to be slow; as a result, profit to the business and pay to the family is never consistent. Both the husband and wife are getting more tired each quarter. They used to love talking with their customers but now just look at them as a necessary evil and complainers. They are getting burned out and really considering closing the business. However, neither of them knows what they would do for a job or how to find one, and they really don't want to work for anyone else. They are stuck.

> *Very few business owners ever define what value they really want to create in their business, nor do they truly attempt to create a valuable business that will sustain itself.*

In the second family business scenario, the husband and wife are starting the business together. They know each of their strengths and weaknesses and have laid out a plan for the roles each person will fill. They sit down weekly to plan the events of the business as well as marketing activities, financial projections and personal schedules. Neither of them wants to be a slave to the business, so they are careful about how they plan their activities. The business startup is expected to be a drain on them personally and financially, but they have a set of financial projections and know what needs to be done to build a profitable business. About one year in, they have saved some of their profits and are ready to bring on an income-producing team member; shortly after that they are looking to outsource some of the accounting functions. This allows the wife to spend more time on marketing and business growth. Their goal is to keep the business for the next 20 years, but they want to reduce their workload in the business by around year 5. They also have a plan for taking 20 percent of the profits each year and putting it aside for an inevitable downturn in the economy or unplanned events. After 10 years in the business, they are at a point where they have consistent revenue and profit growth that has been repeated all of the last eight years. They have built up their retirement savings, purchased land that they rent to the business and have savings. They also have time to spend in the community helping in their children's schools, volunteering in organizations and spending time with friends. Are there still long days at times? Yes. New opportunities arise that create demands on their time, but they make conscious decisions at each point and they have a team of advisors that they use to bounce off new ideas, opportunities and business situations to ensure they are making good decisions.

Which of those two scenarios looks more like your business? Which one do you want your business to look like? Yes, scenario 2 is feasible, practical and implementable. The decision is yours to start making it happen. Or you can continue to stay in scenario 1 and bemoan "Why me?"

Which is it for you?

Family businesses should not define value only in the sense of value to the family or in value to the community, shareholders and employees. The work required to start, operate and build a business has tremendous risk. Yet the owners don't demand a corresponding value in return for the investment of their time and financial resources. I would venture they don't have the same value system when they invest in other things like their house or real estate or the stock market. If those items don't provide a return on investment, they sell, walk away or choose another investment. Why do they not have the same perspective on the value of their own business and their plan to create value? They shortchange themselves in this area.

What needs to happen is to develop a plan to create a more valuable business. The business owners need to determine a plan for returns that are recurring while minimizing the risk of those returns. Here are some questions to consider for creating this view.

Creating a More Valuable View—Rob Slees, Midas Nation

1. *Focus on the business model*
   a. Is this business model one that is solely leveraged off the work of one individual?
   b. Product model
   c. Service model
   d. Others?
2. *Develop a recurring revenue/income stream*
   a. Recurring revenue is the gold of business. Recurring revenue is the portion of a company's revenue that is very likely to continue in the future. This is revenue that is predictable, stable and can be counted on in the future with a high degree of certainty. For example, let's say a software company has a maintenance agreement for its software. Customers pay for software support on a monthly or annual basis in exchange

for support for those services. Without support their ability to operate the software or handle issues would be compromised; therefore this recurring revenue is highly predictable.

3. *Institutionalize the business (management, systems, etc.)*

    a. What systems are in place to allow repeatable operations with a high level of accuracy?

    b. Do you have returning customers, do they need to continue to purchase from you to upgrade, add on to their original purchase. Can you make that process consistent and predictable?

    c. Is management ready to truly manage the business or are they still in the mindset of doing?

CHAPTER 2

Foundations for a Successful Family Business

Assuming the family is involved in this business, you need to step back and create a plan. Run the business like a business. If you don't know what that statement means, then step back and learn. There are many tools to help you in this journey. One recommendation I make to all my clients is for them to enlist what is essentially a board of directors. As the owner of a small family business, you'll probably say, "I can't afford to pay a board." I contend you can't afford not to.

At a minimum you need a team of people you know, like and trust. This team does not necessarily need to have a paid position for every role. You should be associating yourself with people who are running businesses larger than yours. Get to know them. Take them to lunch, breakfast, coffee, whatever works. Ask questions. Don't be a leech, but pick their brains. Be prepared when you meet with them. Determine how you can provide value to them as well. If they are the type of individual you can learn from, they have probably done the same thing and are excited and honored to be able to do the same for someone else.

Dan was a new business owner. He knew he had a lot to learn and really didn't want to make the mistakes he had seen others make. He knew failure was a possibility for a small business, but he also wanted to learn from others. He did some research in his community on the most well-respected and high-growth business owners in the area. He learned a bit about their business (the Internet and social media are wonderful tools). He learned more about their business philosophies and what motivated them. After doing the research (which really didn't take long), Dan called the top individual he wanted to meet and asked him to be a mentor. Dan left a compelling voicemail and Chris called back the next day. They met for lunch. Dan was prepared with the questions he had, the challenges he faced and the opportunity he saw in his business. Chris was so stunned that someone would be interested in his opinion and perspective that they become good friends. They met about every other month. Dan learned and continued to ask questions, and his business reflected his openness to learning.

Run the business like a business.

Dan also had his wife, Cathy, do the same thing. She was in the business with him, but really wanted another female family business owner to mentor her. For each individual it was an opportunity to grow. Chris grew as much from having to think about the questions that Dan asked as Dan did in getting the answers. Dan and Cathy now had outside perspectives and people to laugh, cry, celebrate and grow with. This didn't mean that Dan and Cathy didn't have other advisors on their team (see details below), but it did mean they had been intentional in creating relationships with others who had walked the journey before them and could provide them with sounding boards during their family business journey.

Building Your Advisory Team

Your business's foundation should be built with the expertise of outside strategic advisors. Your core team should include the following:

Legal Counsel—You must understand the legal impact of your decisions. Find a good business lawyer so he or she can steer you clear of many issues that can arise out of having a business. Don't make decisions based just on what you know; trust me, there are many examples of well-intentioned family business owners who have made that assumption and lived to regret it. Some examples of where you might need legal advice include: website naming, company names, patents, business incorporation issues, employee hiring/firing, copyright infringement, business ownership within the family, and estate planning. Additional considerations include:

> *You must understand the legal impact of your decisions.*

- Generational leadership, passing the torch to the kids
- The interplay of familial and business financial portfolios
- Involvement of in-laws/effect of marriage on family businesses
- Terminating business relationships without terminating family bonds
- Taxation issues for family businesses, especially at their inception
- Allocation of responsibilities—and earnings!—within the family structure
- Use of family personal and real property for business purposes and its implications
- The process and implications of expanding beyond blood and marriage with new employees
- When siblings (or parents and children) squabble over the direction of the business

+ Preventative efforts when two family businesses work together or merge

Estate Attorney—Make sure you have:

+ A Revocable Living Trust and/or Last Will and Testament
+ Financial Power of Attorney
+ Medical Power of Attorney
+ Living Will (healthcare directive)
+ HIPAA Authorization

And that you review these documents with your attorney on a regular basis (depending on your age—probably ever 2-3 years).

CPA—More than 25 years ago I had the good fortune to be in management in a business where one of the employee benefits was having a certified public accountant do our personal taxes. (I have never seen that benefit since.) What it taught me was the value of a CPA doing taxes and providing financial advice for the business. The first year she did our taxes, she saved us more than $1,000 in taxes on a deduction that we didn't know existed. This has happened multiple times over the last 25 years as we have continued to have a CPA do our taxes. Also, we have the confidence of our taxes being reviewed by a knowledgeable professional. You can (although I don't recommend it) get away without a CPA doing your personal taxes, but don't try it with your business. When you have a family business, however, the two are intertwined, and what you might pay the CPA is much less than what you can lose from lost deductions or taxes being prepared incorrectly.

Find a CPA you know, like and trust, but make sure he or she knows business—not all CPAs do. I bet I ruffled a few feathers with that statement. Let me clarify: it doesn't mean they don't know taxes or accounting, but not all CPAs really understand business. Business is not black and white; there are many shades of gray that need to be taken into consideration when reviewing the finances of a business. Your CPA should also be part of your advisory team. When you are deciding whether to purchase some equipment, acquire property, buy another business, or take out a loan, call your CPA before you do so. He or she can often help you decide on the best ways to move forward and potentially save you thousands of dollars. It is an investment in your business and your future, so look at it with that perspective. Make sure your CPA is around to do a midyear review as well. Sit down together for an hour, if possible. Provide a set of year-to-date financial statements, and project what you think the balance of the year will look like. This update is critical and can save you taxes and penalties should you assume one thing and find out the reality is another.

A major frustration of CPAs (other than having a box of receipts handed to them on April 10th) is when their clients make financial decisions without consulting them. This can result in clients spending additional money on taxes and CPA costs to unravel decisions that would never had been made if the client had made a simple phone call first.

Insurance Agent—Insurance for your business is critical. There are many examples of businesses that have been underinsured, with the end result being catastrophic. The considerations for a family-owned business can be very different from other business insurance needs. You need to make sure you protect your personal property and investments and keep them separate from the business. Then insure before you need it. Don't be like the proverbial ostrich with your head in the sand saying, "That would never happen." The reality is that it isn't worth taking the chance that there won't be an accident, a client won't get upset with your company, a fire won't happen, an employee won't hurt themselves and the list goes on. Family-owned businesses are especially at risk if personal and business coverage has been intertwined.

Many business owners living in Colorado Springs in 2012 had what we had hoped was a once-in-a-lifetime event. A massive forest fire burned nearly 350 homes and required the evacuation of tens of thousands of people. Many people lost everything. The number of houses was counted, but certainly there were family businesses inside many of those houses that have gone uncounted. If the owners didn't have the proper insurance (and many didn't), their businesses were a total loss.

Review your insurance policies annually.

Many didn't have backups of their records; some who did have backups had stored them in the house, which was now ashes. What happened the following year was just as disastrous—another fire hit and destroyed approximately 486 homes. There were many businesses lost, many family owned, and many will never recover from the devastation of the fire.

Even those businesses that didn't burn were affected when the owners were unable to go back to their place of business for about a week. That meant no paperwork, no ability to answer the phone and no access to tools—unless the owners had thought through "what if" scenarios and had been prepared. Unless they had business interruption insurance, that week cost the owners revenue, not only from the work that did not get done that week but also from what had not been billed the previous week or month that no one remembered took place or work for which there wasn't any paperwork or enough backup to be able to bill the customer. Don't assume it won't happen to you. If it doesn't—fantastic; you will sleep better at night. If it does, then you are prepared. Listen to your insurance agent and if he or she doesn't regularly educate you, change agents.

Here are some tips from an insurance broker of 30 years:

+ If possible, try to purchase a "package policy," one that combines liability, property, loss of income, employee dishonesty, etc.
+ Check out the rates for additional liability; there is usually not much difference between $1 million and $2 million of protection.
+ A business umbrella policy will give additional protection in the

event of a large liability loss whether at your location or involving a business vehicle.

+ Insure your life adequately. If you pass away without adequate protection, your surviving spouse or family member may have to sell the business to a competitor for a fraction of what it's worth.
+ Make sure you purchase replacement cost coverage for your property and that you insure your property for 100 percent of its value; otherwise a co-insurance penalty could apply in the event of a claim.
+ Review your insurance policies annually; what covers your business in year 1 won't cover the business in year 3 or 13. Do not let your insurance policies lapse.

Banker—Your relationship with a banker is critical. Make sure you choose a bank that not only meets your needs today but also meets the anticipated needs of your business three to five years from now. What should you look for in a banker? There is no single answer to that question. However, consider the following:

> *Your relationship with a banker is critical.*

+ What type of banking relationship do you want? Local vs. national bank; personal relationship vs. ATM-only relationship.
+ Do you plan on having offices in multiple states and/or multiple countries? Does your bank need to mirror your business?
+ Will you need lines of credit?
+ Will you need loans for equipment or for acquiring assets like buildings or land?

You can always change banks, but starting out with a plan and establishing a track record with a bank helps when you need the resources. However, when you do need loans or lines of credit, make sure you search around. Not all banks are created equal.

Business Coach—The standard return on investment from an experienced business coach is about 7 to 1. That essentially means that for every dollar you invest, your return is about $7. A business coach helps you think outside the box, challenges you to do more than you think you can and helps with perspective. When you choose your coach, make sure you choose one who has experience with owners of family-owned businesses. The dynamic in family businesses is different from other environments. The interaction of family members within the business can be unique and, in all honesty, trying to many people, so make sure your business coach has a good understanding of family businesses. A good business coach is actually more important than many of the other advisors from the perspective that a coach will know and understand your entire business and can be there to say, "You need to talk to your CPA (your banker, etc.)."

Here are some quotes from my clients regarding coaching:

"Our business is 180 degrees from where it was before Janna. We weren't accustomed to even setting goals. We weren't enjoying work and felt drained by some customers and a couple of employees. To put it simply, we were too nice and needed to start running the business like a business. Janna gave us that push. Today the quality of life at work, and our work itself, is better than ever."

The standard return on investment from an experienced business coach is about 7 to 1.

"As a business owner you may question whether you should spend the money for a business coach. Don't consider it an EXPENSE; consider it an INVESTMENT. Make it a good one, interview a few of them, just like you would a lawyer, CPA, banker etc. Make sure they have the experience you need. Here are the types of testimonials you need to see from a business coach you chose:

"The change in the performance of the business has also had a positive effect on my personal life. Not to make this about me, but I was in a failing marriage after 31 years partially due to the state our business was in. Getting the business in a profitable state helped us repair our marriage, and our marriage is better than it has been in many years."

"Coaching has made a profound impact on my business. Under her guidance, my company's core marketing message now differentiates us from the competition. We've fine-tuned my approach to selling so time isn't wasted on dead-end inquiries, put in place a new sales procedure that will help conversion rates, and new avenues of marketing have been developed that I wouldn't have thought of on my own."

"Janna's insight and experience has brought an immense amount of benefit to our company, which we are only beginning to recognize. She took a culture steeped with fear and complacency and has been able to coach key leaders to push through barriers and ultimately begin to get out of our own way so we could begin to succeed again. We are now working together as a team without backbiting and critical talk. We are becoming a positive environment with engaged employees. As a result, our clients are happier, our product is better and our profits are on the rise."

"I have often been asked by other business owners how long I plan to utilize Janna business coaching services. My answer is always the same: either until I decide I don't want my business to grow any more or until I decide that I don't want to make any more money than I currently am. She very quickly went from being a variable expense that we weren't sure we could justify to a fixed expense that we feel we cannot do without."

Find a coach who meets your personal and business needs. Here are some basic questions to help you select a coach:

+ What is their experience level?
+ Have they run a business?
+ Are they someone who can hold you accountable?
+ Do you like them? You don't necessarily need to get along with the coach (although it helps), but they do need the ability to listen and push you in a way that will create results.

- How well do they run their business? Are they congruent to what they coach?
- What do their references say about them and the results from their coaching?

Other advisors that should be in your contact list include:

- **Payroll Company**—Depending on your circumstances, you might need one as soon as you have two or three employees. They can save you a tremendous amount of time.
- **Business Broker**—A business broker helps in the valuation and selling of a business. They have a great deal of knowledge about how to best sell a business, preparing for sale and making the sale happen.
- **Certified Financial Planner (CFP)/Investment Advisor**—This person should be able to advise you on a combination of personal and business matters.

Business Advisory Board

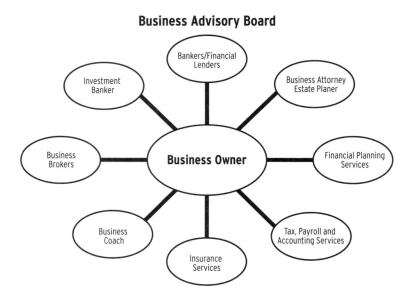

Building Your Business Knowledge

Here are some of the key areas all business owners need to understand:

- Do you know how to read financial statements? You don't need to be a CPA, but you should know some basics:
  - Total revenue (aka income or sales)
  - Cost of goods sold—What it costs you to deliver your product or service
  - Overhead—What it costs you to keep the business operating even if you don't make one cent in revenue
  - Profit for the period—Month, quarter, year
  - Balance sheet—The true picture of the value of your business
- Do you know how to negotiate with:
  - Lawyers
  - Bankers
  - CPAs
  - Vendors
- Do you know how to buy products that you use?
- How is inventory assessed and valued (if you have it)?
- What makes up WOW customer service and raving fans as defined earlier?
- What does it take to sell?
- What are your key performance indicators (KPIs)? Here are some examples:
  - Bank reconciliation
  - Weekly cash flow forecast
  - Aged debtors and creditors
  - Monthly profit and loss statement
  - Monthly balance sheet
  - Annual budgets
  - Break-even analysis
  - Company-specific KPIs
  - Team—and employee-specific KPIs

- How do you know you are getting a return on your investment (ROI) for your marketing dollars?
- What skeletons are in your closet that your advisors need to know and understand? Yes, we all have them, so stop sticking your head in the sand.

One strong recommendation—and this is for all business owners but really critical for family businesses—is to keep personal and business totally separate from a financial perspective. Let me say this again: Keep personal and business totally separate from a financial perspective. That means separate bank accounts, and I even recommend separate banks. Have separate credit cards as well. Don't pay for personal expenses with your business card and business expenses with your personal card. Mixing the two will cost you money—for your CPA who has to try to separate the charges—and time—as you try to remember what you purchased with which funds.

A business had not kept things separate and had not filed taxes for about five years. (Don't laugh; it is not as uncommon as you think.) It essentially took the owners two-plus years of time and tens of thousands of dollars to clean up the mess. They had to reconstruct everything on top of running the business, keeping their family life balanced and dealing with other aspects of life. More than once at 11 p.m. the husband and wife would sit on the floor at home going through old receipts and categorizing between business and personal and what the charge was for. It was not fun, and although their business grew during that time, the business was affected and the stress was phenomenal. Time was spent on tax cleanup that could have been spent with family or growing their business even more. It impacted all aspects of their lives until everything was cleaned up and paid off. This was one task that could not be delegated; they were the only ones who understood if each receipt was business or personal.

Keep personal and business totally separate from a financial perspective.

The moral of the story: Don't combine business and personal finances and don't get behind; the end result will be more painful than keeping up. In other words: Don't procrastinate—that frog you need to eat will not get any easier to enjoy. There is an old Mark Twain saying: **"Eat a live frog every morning, and nothing worse will happen to you the rest of the day."** This is a simple time management and procrastination tip. Do the worst possible thing you have to do every day first thing in the morning—you day will only get better once that "thing" is done.

This applies to finances and all other aspects of your life.

Take advantage of the free resources that are available in your community. Understand that they are free; the people who provide this assistance do not receive payment, you often meet with them only once or twice, and they often don't have the full picture—usually because you haven't told them all your family secrets—but they can be incredibly useful and can help you understand and find out more about the resources in your community.

A couple of examples are the Small Business Association (SBA), Service Corps of Retired Executives (SCORE) and Small Business Development Centers (SBDC). All of these organizations offer free counseling in a number of areas including finance, legal issues, marketing, banking, bookkeeping and sales. Take advantage of these resources. Most of the staff are knowledgeable and can assist with specific aspects of your business. I have volunteered with the SBDC for a number of years, and it is very rewarding. The impact the organization has on businesses is huge.

There are numerous resources that can help you as a business owner, but they can't be of use to you unless you reach out to them. Business owners often wait too long before they seek assistance. It seems to be a combination of thought processes that prevent people from asking for help. Don't fall into these traps:

+ **Ego**—"I can do it; I don't need help." Guess what? *Everyone* needs help. In fact, the most profitable, most well-run businesses are run by owners who constantly ask questions and seek help.

+ **Shame**—"I don't want anyone to know the hole I have dug for myself and my family." It will come out at some point, and as John Maxwell states in his book *Failing Forward*, "Success is measured by your perception of and response to failure. Every person fails. Every business owner fails at some point. It is only with failure that you can truly be a success. This may sound harsh, but get over it, figure out how big the hole is, what can be done about it, LEARN from it and move on. I love the old song that says: Pick yourself up, dust yourself off and start all over again!"

+ **Fear**—"I don't want to know what trouble I am really in." As business leader, coach, speaker and trainer Paul Martinelli said, "To live a creative life, we must lose our fear of being wrong." A business was owned by a mother and daughter. They provided childcare to the community and accomplished their service in an extraordinary way. Unfortunately, the relationship between mother and daughter was often confrontational. The mother eventually ended up firing her daughter and running the business herself. The business started to grow as the marketing was working and new families were interested in the service. However, the mother knew she was behind in paying bills, so she stopped checking her voicemail. Her fear of what the messages would say was so great that she was unable to listen even to gather voicemails from new families seeking her services. The end result was that the marketing activity was of no value when fear kept her from following up. The end result was a closed and bankrupt business, employees out of work and another business not fulfilling its potential. FEAR is False Expectations Appearing Real. Her fear was people calling for payment of late bills. Reality is her voicemail included those very families that could have taken care of the creditors and kept the business afloat. What are your fears?

+ **Didn't know**—"I did not realize there were resources out there to help me." If you are going to own your own business, you must read, be aware, listen and not stick your head in the sand. You *must* be *always* learning. In this age of computers and the Internet, there are many resources to help you; not knowing is not acceptable. The challenge is to ask better questions so when you do seek out help you get the right answers, not the answers you want. There will always be things you don't know, didn't understand, didn't consider. As a business owner, try to minimize the effects of not knowing by creating a plan for learning.

> › You can learn by listening—Always have a CD in your car or a download on your iPod. This is a program called Traffic University. Pick a topic and listen to a CD or download as you drive.

> › Learn by reading daily. Read about business, leadership, marketing, finance, managing, psychology and many other topics. Even 15 minutes per day will radically change your perception and knowledge about your business. For a no-cost alternative to buying books, check your library's selection of business books. One of my clients simply didn't like to read business books, so I started her with *Think Big* by Dr. Robert Anthony. It is a collection of thoughts regarding business and was a place for her to start. Start somewhere with your reading and DO IT!

> › Meet regularly with other business owners. Find business owners with businesses larger than yours, ask questions, take them to lunch, pick their brain, and understand what they did and what they would do differently. Then be open to doing the same with other business owners who are younger than you in your business venture. Notice I said business venture, not age; age is not relevant here. A 35-year-old business owner who has owned his or her business for seven years has a great deal of wisdom to share with a 50-year-old business owner who is just starting out. Humble yourself and ask questions. Make sure that all family members do the same. Meet with other owners of family-owned businesses in noncompeting space. Be specific with your questions and learn.

> Attend conferences on your industry, business or family businesses. Just the process of getting away from your business will give you much needed perspective. I once heard a coach to Fortune 100 executives state that he insists his clients take a vacation every six to eight weeks. Those vacations generated millions and millions of dollars' worth of new ideas, new potential and perspective. You must regularly get away, recharge your batteries and allow yourself time to think.

+ **MBA know-it-all**—This is my favorite. "I don't need help; I have an MBA." Sorry, but having an MBA doesn't guarantee you won't go out of business. The reality is that earning an MBA often teaches you the book learning, not the real-world aspect of running a business, especially a small family business. It may prepare you for a job at a company that wants what is taught at business school, but it seldom prepares you for starting your own company. I have encountered many family business owners who don't believe they need help because they have an MBA and they know how to do the business thing. I have also encountered just as many business owners who have been humbled by losing their business because they thought they learned it all while earning their MBA. This statement may not be popular with business schools, but I will stand behind it. A number of schools have started entrepreneurial programs—which is fantastic—but they still often fall short of the reality of business ownership. Don't fall into the trap. Understand that the more you know, the more you realize you have lots more to learn and need help learning it as quickly as possible.

> Those with MBAs should be the most open to learning and to understanding how much more they need to learn. They have gone through the classes and have seen how much more there is out there to learn. Unfortunately that doesn't seem to be the case. An MBA business owner who I met with owned a honey farm. The more we talked, the more I grew concerned about the future of his business. Yet he was so closed to any

discussion that I ended the conversation shortly after it started. I followed the business for a while and then noticed it was no longer around. I was not surprised.

Here are two stories that emphasize that anything can happen and that sometimes you just can't see what is needed.

At the height of the 2007–2008 recession and housing bust, a realtor wanted a loan for TV advertising. A couple of us counseled her against it, but helped her complete the paperwork and submit the application. I would have bet money she would not have received the loan, but to my surprise she did. Unfortunately, She went through with the advertising and spent the money. The end result was no increase in her sales and no return on investment. It is an unfortunate result that happens way too often. Now don't read into this that TV advertising is wrong. It isn't; however, it must have the following elements just like any other advertising medium:

- A marketing plan with an end goal in mind
- Ways to test and measure results
- A definitive target
  - › Do they watch TV (or use the medium through which you are advertising)?
  - › Does your client need a relationship with you before they buy and will this ad get them to at least pick up the phone to call you?
  - › What is your process, once they have called, to ensure you transition them to the next step in your sales process?
  - › Do you **have** a sales process?
  - › A plan to revise and continually strive for more successful results.

Dale couldn't focus on his carpet cleaning business to move it ahead. He was always tired. In our first session we worked through creating a marketing plan. His homework was to take three action items and start to make them happen. Our second session lasted about 10 minutes. He had gotten nothing done because he was always tired. After some discussion, I advised him to get some sleep—more than three hours per night would be a good start. He thought that was a great idea and was ready to put that into practice. I only saw him one other time after those free sessions. He was still in the business. It wasn't really growing and was barely paying the bills. His wife still worked at a fast-food restaurant to help make ends meet and also worked with him in the business. Lack of a plan, discipline and follow-through led to a mediocre business that was barely making ends meet and constantly tired business owners.

Now the recommendations may sound simple and obvious, yet my purpose for the stories is this: Never give up—even if others don't believe in you—and remember that no question, issue or challenge is too small. Sometimes we just can't see the forest for the trees.

Building Your Business Plan

This is probably contrary to every piece of advice you have ever been given about starting a business, but if you don't need to go to a bank or the SBA for a loan, don't spend days, weeks and months writing a business plan. I have seen many business owners with wonderful business plans that they took months to complete. When we first meet, they take it off the shelf, blow 3 inches of dust off the cover and hand it to me. They spent weeks and months and often thousands of dollars preparing it. They fretted over the wording and all the sections. They then said it was complete, opened the business and never looked at it again. However, they were now able to check off the box that said they had a business plan.

I had the opportunity to meet with some female engineers one evening. They had an interest in starting some businesses and wanted to know what they should consider. One of the women had written a business plan almost three years ago and still hadn't opened the business.

Her fear of opening the business kept her from acting. By the time she really considered taking action and doing it, so much time had passed that others had already opened a similar type of business. Her window of opportunity to have a unique business and market share had closed.

She probably had the best business plan around, but the best business plan by itself won't get you a real business nor generate revenue or the resulting profit. Action is required, risk is required, and getting out of your comfort zone is also critical. Don't get stuck in the planning and never take the action required to make it happen. Make a plan of what you will get accomplished every day and stick to it. If needed, go with what one of my former business clients did when he wanted to implement a company-wide software system on a short schedule. He implemented a 24-hour rule: All decisions needed to be made within 24 hours of the decision being required. They didn't have time for committees and hand wringing over decisions. This accomplished two goals for his implementation—actually making decisions rather than putting them off and creating momentum. If writing your business plan can start that process for your business, then the momentum you create will benefit you and your business forever.

> *Don't get stuck in the no planning zone and run the business by the seat of your pants.*

Yet don't get stuck in the no planning zone and run the business by the seat of your pants. Lack of a plan will get you in just as much trouble as a dusty, unused plan. Lay out a plan to accomplish the goals and objectives for your business. It must have the basics including:

+ Marketing
+ Financials
+ Product
+ Sales process
+ Customer focus
+ Team
+ Leveraging through systems

Having a foundational business plan is important, and there are many classes available to help you create one. (The SBDC and SCORE are great at helping to build the basics.) Many small family-owned businesses will never apply for a big SBA loan. They might receive a line of credit from a bank but not a loan. If you don't need a big loan, then sit down with your key advisors and spend a measured amount of time (days and not weeks or months) determining the plan for your business.

What is needed is a living, breathing document that you use every week, quarter and year to determine your focus, direction and plan for the activities that run your business. This document must be reviewed on a regular basis and updated *at least quarterly*. The foundation may have all the tenets of a business plan, but it also generates an action plan that keeps you and the business focused. If you are not updating the plan on a regular basis, then it slowly dies and becomes useless. The business, the goals and your objectives start being whipped around by the wind of emotion, new ideas and economic conditions. A strong one-year operational goals list, teamed with a detailed 90-day action plan will keep the focus on the end goal for your business. It will also provide the family the direction it needs to accomplish the critical objectives.

Now with all that said, business plans are important and below are some basic recommendations.

A business plan can be as short as a couple of pages or as long as 100+ pages. Your purpose for creating the plan, the complexity of your business, and the amount of information required to demonstrate that your plan is sound are all factors. A 10- to 15-page document is sufficient for small businesses preparing for startup, growth, transition or sale.

Business plan contents vary; however, there are essential elements that need to be addressed:

- **Business Profile**—Description of your business, goals, operations, products, services, markets and competitive advantage.
- **Internal/External Environments**—Research regarding potential customers and competitors to determine the demand for your

products or services, assess current economic conditions and industry growth, and understand emerging technologies. Research should include:

> > A SWOT analysis (**s**trengths, **w**eaknesses, **o**pportunities, and **t**hreats)
> > Competitive advantage—What is your unique selling proposition (USP)? That is, what makes you different from everyone else?
> > > Who will buy from me?
> > > Why will they buy from me?
> > > How will I provide what they buy?

+ **Execution Plan**—Includes mission/purpose, goals, vision, values and execution strategy, such as:
  > SMART objectives (**s**pecific, **m**easureable, **a**ttainable, **r**elevant and **t**ime-bound)
  > Performance measurements and tactical actions
+ **Financial Pro Formas**—A 12-month cash flow forecast and a profit and loss forecast for a minimum of a year and preferably two years.

COACH'S CORNER
Your Business Plan

+ Keep it simple; include and monitor only the most critical factors, competencies and priorities that drive your business.
+ Don't spend months developing the plan.
+ Include management and key employees in the analysis.

Remember, the best business plans are concise and practical. The purpose is to attract investors and other funding sources and to keep you on track toward your core business objectives.

Be Sure to Review Your Plan Regularly

Business plans provide a business direction and a template for execution. A plan can ensure your business success, maximize value and provide action timelines to reach desired targets. It builds commitment and credibility, and convinces others that you know what you are doing and where your business is heading.

Your business plan should also help you set goals—from three- to five-year strategic goals down to daily goals. The goals in your **three- to five-year strategic plan** should describe what the company as a whole needs to achieve to be successful over the life of the strategic plan. These goals should be important and apply to the entire organization, and the links between the goals and company success should be clear and obvious. The goals should be measurable. Goals in your strategic plan can be either results oriented or process oriented. Here are examples of results-oriented goals:

+ Increase share price by 6 percent
+ Increase market share by 12 percent
+ Increase return on capital investments by 15 percent
  Here are some examples of more process-oriented goals:
+ Reduce employee turnover by 15 percent
+ Bring two new products to market
+ Register five new patents

Your business plan should also address **one-year operational goals**. These goals are the short-term tactics designed to achieve the company's long-term strategy. Operational goals lay out details of what must be accomplished. For example, if a company's strategy is to corner 20 percent of the market for a particular line of products within two years, you may have detailed steps to lock in prices and quantities with suppliers, find the most efficient way to manufacture the product and assemble enough merchandise to meet projected sales. Assembly details might be

How to Set Goals

- Three to Five Years–Strategic
- One Year–Operations
- 90 Days–Results
- Monthly–Financials
- Weekly–Plans
- Daily–Discipline

50 percent of the desired weekly production during a one-week training period, and then an increase in production of 10 percent per week until the operational goal is attained regularly.

A **90-day plan** becomes the critical piece to achieving the one-year operational and three- to five-year strategic goals. The 90-day results goal breaks down into smaller steps what will actually be accomplished in the next 90 days. Let's use a simple example that is more personal than business: In one year you want to be healthier than you are today. One aspect of improving your health is losing 20 pounds. Thus, the goal is to lose 20 pounds. The goal doesn't include the details required to make that happen. As most fitness coaches will tell you, it is the detailed plan that makes it happen. For example:

1. Determine when in your schedule you will work out.
2. Decide where you will work out.
3. Choose what types of equipment and activities you will use to achieve the targeted weight goal.
4. Determine what dietary modifications are required to achieve the targeted weight.

Now you are ready to determine what the workout will look like. To meet your goal, you might need to work out for an hour seven days a week. This is probably not going to happen unless you have become tremendously disciplined and are ready for a major lifestyle change. The real change comes when you make the daily changes required to accomplish this goal. You may actually start with something as simple as one hour per week to start creating the habit. The habit and the resulting discipline are what start you on your path to making the lifelong change.

Now let's take that concept to business. The three- to five-year strategic goal is to grow profitability by 10 percent each year. The one-year operational goal is to determine which products are not at the targeted gross profit, i.e., they may not sell well or may not be priced well.

The 90-day goal might be a detailed review of the gross profit margins on all products.

Financials should be reviewed on a **monthly** basis. This means looking at your financial statements (profit/loss, cash flow forecast, sales forecast, balance sheet). Also each

Those who fail to plan, plan to fail.

month you should take a couple of hours to review last month's accomplishments and plan for next month. Look at your 90-day goals and determine how are you progressing, what has changed and what needs to be adjusted to meet those goals.

Weekly and **daily** goals that break down the products or product lines to be reviewed. If there are 100 products, then you might examine 10 products per week, which might take 30 minutes per week rather than one five-hour time block.

Financials should be reviewed on a Monthly basis. This means looking at your financial statements (profit/Loss, Cash flow forecast, sales forecast Balance Sheet). Also once per month you should take a couple of hours and review the accomplishments of last month and plan for next month. Look at your 90 day goals, how are you progressing, what has changed, what needs to be adjusted to meet those goals.

Ben Franklin has been quoted as saying "By failing to prepare, you are preparing to fail." This is often adapted to "Those who fail to plan, plan to fail." What are you planning for?

If you don't know how to go about developing these plans and goals, then get a business coach to help you with the process. The following are some examples of the foundational areas you must address not only in starting the business but also on a regular basis. Some of these items you may look at quarterly and some annually depending on the business.

+ Who is your target market? And if the word "any" or "every" is in the description, then start over and determine your actual target market.
+ What is your product or service (i.e., what are people going to pay you for)?
+ How do you need to price your product or service to make a profit? (Make sure you include paying yourself in this calculation; I would say 80 percent of small business owners I meet with say they are making money but don't pay themselves; therefore I disagree that they are making money. See chapter 4 for how to look at this in a different way.)
+ Do you have an annual budget projecting the next 12 months, monthly profit and loss statements and an annual profit and loss statement? What about a balance sheet?
+ What cash flow do you need? You need a rolling cash flow forecast (looking out into the future) for a minimum of three months.
+ What is your target market? Who is going to buy and why will they buy from you? And are they willing to pay a price that will allow you to make money?
+ What are the skill sets of the people involved in the business? Here is where it is critical that you are honest with yourself and others. If you hate selling, then either learn to stop hating it or get someone who loves to sell involved. The reality is that if you are a business owner, the most important skill you *must* learn is how to sell. If you are unwilling to learn, then don't start the business— you will waste time and money and create stress trying to make it successful. There is a small percentage of business owners (less

than 5 percent) who can become successful without recognizing the critical nature of being able to sell and learning how to do it well.

+ What does servicing your customers or clients mean? Not what is the product, but how will you create an extraordinary experience that will get them coming back and referring others to your business?

+ Have you created a marketing plan? This plan should account for at least 10 ways to market your business on a regular basis.

+ What kind of culture will you create? One of the foundations of a business is the culture. Who are you? Why do people want to work for you? Are you rigid? That is, must employees show up at 8 a.m. and not 8:01 and leave at 5 p.m., not 4:59? Are you fun to work with? What do you define as fun? (Not everyone defines fun the same.) There are hundreds of words, phrases and ideas of what makes up your culture. If you are just starting out, the easy part is figuring out what you want to be. If you have been in business for a while, you need to determine your current culture and what you want it to be. Changing culture can be difficult, but it is worth the rewards when the process is complete. Entire books have been written on culture; a couple I suggest are:
   › *Good to Great* by Jim Collins
   › *Start with Why: How Great Leaders Inspire Everyone to Take Action* by Simon Sinek

Opportunities are ahead if you heed the wisdom of your business advisors. Yet the business advice people often look toward is what I call Hopium: I hope next year will be better. I hope my revenue will grow. I hope, I hope, I hope. Jim Rohn says that "a wish is a dream without a plan." Hope is no different. "I don't have time to plan" is the mantra I hear constantly. You don't have the time not to. Let me ask you a few questions:

- Do you work more hours than you want to?
- Are you getting paid what you want (notice I didn't say "need"; I said "want")?
- Are you constantly reacting to situations around you and perceive you have no time?
- Is there never enough cash at the end of the month?
- Does worrying about the "what if's" keep you up at night?

These are just a few of the questions that indicate you must start making the time to plan. Here is what planning has accomplished for some of my clients:

- One client was able to see the reality of the company's cash position in a few months and adjust spending so there was cash available at the end of each month and no deficit.
- Another client planned in detail for the start of a new sister company and within nine months was profitable, which was three months ahead of schedule.
- A business owner I mentored was able to find time to truly be a CEO by stopping and planning rather than reacting. He was then able to put systems into place to save himself hours every week, thus allowing for more time to work on other areas of interest.
- Another business coaching client was able through planning to put the proper team in place for a new project that was acquired.

Do you make plans with your family? Do you sometimes not go to activities with your children because you have another commitment? Take the lessons you've learned about creating business plans and goals and try planning on a family basis at least once per month. Go over calendars, understand what is going on and have the kids participate. Two things will happen: The family will run smoother and you will teach your kids the value of planning. Now what will that look like as a legacy?

So STOP, eliminate the excuses and set aside the day. Get out of the office, turn off your phone and glance back at last year and plan for next year. Everyone will thank you for it.

Here is a concept for running your business:
Revenue is Vanity,
Profit is Reality and
Cash is King.
Where is your King Plan?

CHAPTER 3

The Upside of the Family Business

A printing company was owned by three siblings. They had purchased it from their dad a number of years prior. Although the industry has been challenged given the move to e-books and email marketing and away from printing, they are successful and supporting essentially four families: the three siblings and their dad, as they continue to pay him for the business.

During my interview with them, I asked them a question: What was one piece of advice they would give to potential family business owners? In unison, they all said, "DON'T." In other words, don't go into business with family. Although they are happy to be in business together, the stress, challenges and struggles prompted them to advise others not to do it. The thought of owning a business is glamorous; the challenge lies in the implementation.

Now with that said, none of them would ever think of leaving the business. They have all grown in their knowledge of business and life.

They love what they do and see the value to their families and the community but understand that it is a calling that works well for only some families. After the recommendation of *don't*, I asked for their second piece of advice and received many suggestions that are critical for running a business with family members:

+ Be open and communicate. Talk to each other, not at each other.
+ Be respectful.
+ Document everything you plan on doing with the business and have business discussions upfront.
+ Don't take things personally and don't make comments of a personal nature.
+ Determine your exit strategy before you need to use it.
+ Create your estate plan. It is easier to do that when you're young than after wealth has been created and there is a fight looming.
+ Don't be afraid to discuss difficult issues. It is better to clear the air than to let something brew and not be addressed.

What is the Upside?

Acceptance: The family knows you, accepts you and loves you for who you are. Notice I didn't say like. Families don't always like each other, yet there is a foundational love and acceptance as you grow learn and develop in the business.

Opportunities: The family business provides the opportunity to work in areas and situations that may not always be possible otherwise. The intorudction spoke of the Perkins family. David as a 4th generation family member may not hve had the opportunity to run an auto dealership at age 29 if he wasn't family. He is great at running the business and succeeding, but that opportunity and that of the previous generations may not have been possible otherwise.

Flexibility: Many if not most family business owners have far more flexibility than the general employee workforce. The ability to choose to work part time, full time or "your" time is possible. Those options may not be acceptable in other work environments. One family which had a husband/wife ownership planned to pass the business to two brothers. One was still in college. The one brother was able to work 1 day per week, get experience, get paid, go to school and come and go as his schedule allowed. That is flexibility. He still had responsibilities but received the experience that he might not have gotten elsewhere if Mom and Dad didn't own the business.

Time with Family: This can also be a downside, yet the joy of family business ownership is being able to work with family. They know you, know how you think, know your strengths and weaknesses. They are often your mirror. They look like you, act like you and that can be fun, energizing and comforting. The stories at family gatherings is what books *Be open and communicate. Talk to each other, not at each other.* are mode up of and where memories are created. Enjoy, share accept and grow in the family business as it is a great way to be in business and generate wealth and legacy. I love watching families that like to spend time with each other. You can tell the depth of the relationships. They finish each other sentences, thoughts and dreams. It is a wonderful thing to behold and one that the business can only grow to compound and strengthen.

Financial Security: When done right the family business can create that financial legacy that is passed down from generation to generation. There are many financial advantages. Make sure you are taking advantage of them. Ask your CPA. She will know them and how to best utilize those advantages to benefit your family and the generations to come.

Fun: Your business has the opportunity to bring tremendous fun to your life. It is work, yet when you work with those you love, then you can truly have that freedom of expression and resulting fun. One family business every year had a "board meeting" in Florida. They made the meeting in January, went away, accomplished the business at hand, and annual planning, review of the past year and then played. How does it get better?

Personal Growth: Often the only people who will be truly honest with you is family. That can come as a blessing and a curse, yet when given properly and taken properly that honesty can make you the person you need to be. My favorite quote is: "Hell on earth is seeing the person I could have been." Without that input you might not be the person you need to grow into. Employees are often unable or afraid to provide you honest feedback in fear of losing their job. Family will say it like it is. As a result your own personal growth can be exponential, and more targeted. Personal growth will make your life better where ever you venture.

> *Spend time with your spouse every week away from work. Make it a rule to not discuss work in any way.*

Team: You aren't alone. You have a family team to strategize with, gorw with, cry on, rejoice to, celebrate with. Business owners can feel and be a very very lonely journey. Unless you are a family, they you are traveling on a family business journey together. The lonliness is shared with others which makes the journey much more enjoyable.

Support: There are times when the mountain looks impassible. The work load is overwhelming, the competition fierce. Yet in the family business you have the support and encouragement of your family. I like to climb 14'rs. For those of you who don't live in Colorado that means I like to climb mountains that are over 14,000 feet in elevation. We climbed Mt. Princeton, which was a tough climb for a multitude of reasons (like accidentally not following the path, lots of granite rocks that required climbing with hands and feet). My husband and part business owner on his "fun" day off really showed me the value of encouragement. When I was close to giving up, he encouraged me by saying, "we are almost there". When he was getting exhausted, I encouraged him. We made it to the top. It was awesome, phenomenal and once again showed me the power of family.

This happens in our business life and that support is often the reason for the success in the family business.

Here are some other recommendations to consider, especially if you and your spouse work together:

1. **Spend time with your spouse every week away from work.** Make it a rule to not discuss work in any way. You must maintain your life outside of the business in order to attain balance and be interesting. It will also help your business to not be quite so one-dimensional.

2. **Take a day once a quarter and get away.** It doesn't need to be expensive—a bike ride and a picnic don't cost much, but they allow you to recharge your batteries. Again, make it a rule to not discuss work (or money) in any way.

3. **Take a vacation with the family once a year.** Get away for one week (at least) with no work, no interruptions and no technology (I know that is heresy). Again, the vacation doesn't need to be expensive, but everyone needs time to reacquaint themselves with the family, find out what is going on and create memories. If you didn't grow up taking vacations, make it a point to start. If you say you can't get away from the business, you need to figure out how anyway; you have a year to make it happen. I can already hear the excuses: I don't have time, I don't have the money, I don't know where to go or what to do. *Stop it* and just make it happen. You will probably live longer.

4. **Create a gratitude journal.** Write down every day what you are thankful for. Have a page for all the things you are thankful for about your spouse. Then when you have a bad day, go read that page. After six months, show your spouse all the things you have

written down. I guarantee it will change how both of you feel about each other.

5. **Stop trying to change your family.** Let's start with your spouse: You married them as they are—accept them for who they are and stop wasting your time and energy making them change. If change takes place, it will be their decision in their time frame. With the help of your gratitude journal, start looking for their strengths and use those strengths in the business. When that happens, your business will reflect the joy of someone playing to their strengths. Or one of you get *out* of the business, hire someone else to do the job you or your spouse was doing and start rebuilding your life. For siblings: It has been said countless times "How did such different children come from the same parents?" It happens; be thankful you are not all alike and figure out how to build on your strengths. One way to do this is through a book called *Strengths-Finder 2.0* by Tom Rath.

6. **Get advice from someone outside the family.** Someone who can help to navigate business relationships. A good business coach can help to facilitate the business environments and relationships, and help all the individuals grow and build on their strengths. That usually will not happen without outside assistance, like someone from your advisory board

COACH'S CORNER
The Upside

Remember the upsides to the family business. It may be necessary to repeat them on a regular basis, but they are critical.

- Acceptance
- Opportunities
- Flexibility
- Team
- Financial Security
- Fun
- Personal Growth
- Support

CHAPTER 4

The Downside of the Family Business

All businesses entail risk. Financial, personal and legal risks abound. You must have an appetite for risk; otherwise life and business will not be enjoyable. It is that risk (as well as a few other factors) that creates tension in the family business. My mom was not the risk taker in our family. My dad always had a new idea or new opportunity and saw potential in many things. Mom was wonderfully supportive of Dad, yet I knew that the risks he took created a level of tension between them. He took a huge risk when he put down $1,000—essentially all their savings—to purchase the mobile home park and then quit his job. Fortunately for them it worked out well. If it hadn't, the end result would have been financial ruin. They were both wise and understood financials so they were always aware of their financial standing. They also both worked in the business, so they essentially leveraged their time as they started out.

Yet it doesn't always work that way.

Scott and Tracey had a business, but Tracey wasn't really involved. It was really Scott's, and their two sons worked in the business after school and during school breaks. Scott liked the fun of starting the business, getting it going, negotiating and making things happen, but he didn't really enjoy the day-to-day reality of running a business. As time moved on, they wanted to sell because Scott was tired and he no longer enjoyed many facets of the business. However, as much as they tried they had not been able to sell the business, which put the family in a rough situation and forced Tracey to begin looking for work, creating stress that led to them contemplating divorce. The business was becoming a burden and one that they were unlikely to exit from without essentially closing it down.

When Divorce Happens

Divorce can be catastrophic for the business. When both spouses are equally involved in the operation of the business, the divorce impacts not only the business but also the clients and employees. Fortunately I haven't worked with many business owners who wound up divorcing. Couples often come to me when their business is affecting the marriage, but coaching often resolves their business issues, which in turn provides a

The stress of running a business often surfaces in relationships.

new perspective and resolve to address their marital issues. I did have one couple as a client that I strongly felt if they didn't change the way their business was run, the end result would be a divorce. The marriage and the business are thriving to this day.

The stress of running a business often surfaces in relationships. The day-in and day-out demands of delivering the product or service combined with the lack of relationship building and not being able to get away from the business takes its toll. Running a business with your spouse is essentially a 24/7 operation. Both parties live, eat and sleep the business—both its good and bad aspects. The business is often like a mistress. One spouse often looks at the business as the "other woman" or "other man" in their lives. When business demands attention, it gets it. When family demands attention, the leftover time, energy and emotion are pretty scarce.

Another challenge comes from exposing weaknesses. In a marriage, although most dirty laundry is aired between the couple, the true strengths and weaknesses of an individual aren't necessarily spoken about. I know my husband isn't great at socializing, yet we make it work and I don't force the situation unless necessary. However, the fact that he doesn't like networking, selling and that level of socializing could be catastrophic for a business if that is the role that is needed at a particular time. That then creates stress on all aspects of the business and married life. What I see with families who work together is that home becomes less of a safe haven and more about what didn't happen at work. You aren't fulfilling your responsibilities either at work or on the home front. You can extrapolate that example into many different areas—the ability to handle finances, multitask, address employees, deal with confrontation, create a vision for the business, get things done and the list goes on. This stress comes home if not handled correctly, and the marriage may not be able to take that stress.

Now if the end result is still that divorce happens, then step back and figure out the business aspects. Unfortunately what often happens is the business fails. I don't have any statistics, but I do see the result of failure in small business when divorce happens. One couple that I knew actually got divorced after they purchased a franchise but before the doors to the business opened. Unfortunately, the business was doomed almost before it started. The conflicts were significant. They tried hard to make it work, but after about two years, the doors were shut and they both moved on. Although all the specifics weren't shared, I wonder if it would not have been more financially viable for them to not have opened the business at all. When the marriage is on the rocks before the business opens, there are obvious issues that will always carry over into the day-to-day operations.

Therefore my advice is to enter the family business the same way you would a partnership with someone other than a spouse. Have a legal document created that indicates what will happen upon the dissolving of the marriage, such as who gets the business, etc. A good lawyer can do a great job of asking the right questions. I would suggest finding a business lawyer as they understand the challenges of dissolving a business and therefore know what to allow for in creating the documents. Yes, this is a difficult topic and one that most married couples are not willing to discuss; however, I strongly recommend having such an agreement in place. This is very important in creating your business; don't make assumptions—you may regret it.

Other aspects of how divorce affects a family business are discussed in chapter 12.

One other piece of advice: Be careful creating a business that is an equal 50/50 partnership whether with a family member or a non-family member. Issues can end up as stalemates. One person must have the final say on decisions about how the business is run. If that is not the case, then too much time is spent making sure the other party is OK with decisions. Now I am not saying don't communicate and become a dictator. But one person needs to be in charge. It goes back to the old saying that a camel is a horse designed by a committee—or a 50/50 partnership! Yet some of you will still form—or already have—a 50/50 partnership business structure. With that in mind, here are some suggestions:

1. You still need to determine who is in charge and get that documented. One of my clients (that wasn't family owned) did a great job at this. Each owned 50 percent, but one of them was the president and had all the final say in running the business. The other partner was consulted on all critical items but didn't need to worry about reviewing every decision.

2. There must be a strong element of trust in any of these situations. Trust does not mean either abdication (walking away from

knowing what is going on) or lack of checks and balances. As the story in chapter 3 of the three siblings indicated, document everything you plan to do with the business, think it through, plan it out and do this on a regular basis.

3. Most likely one of you will have a strong personality, so you will need to create checks and balances on how communication will take place among people with different communication styles. This will be addressed in more depth in chapter 13.

Illness or Death in the Family

In the journey of life, situations occur that impact our ability to focus on life, let alone business. Emily, her parents, three brothers, three cousins and two sets of uncles and aunts all worked in a manufacturing business. They had about 10 other employees, but most of the responsibility of running the business fell on the shoulders of the family. Then disaster struck: Mom was diagnosed with cancer. She had been the lifeblood and bond for the whole family all these years. The cancer took its toll on Mom and everyone else in the family. They no longer cared about delivering orders, servicing customers, selling product or growing the business. They wanted to be at her side during the last weeks and months prior to her death. That is exactly where they needed to be, but the business could not run without the family. No plan had been put in place to allow for the entire family to essentially be unavailable for weeks at a time. Orders weren't being filled, deposits weren't being made and materials weren't being ordered.

What should be done to address a situation where the owners of a family business are devastated by a crisis? There are no easy answers, but be aware that such a situation affects not only the family but also employees, vendors, customers and all other relationships.

COACH'S CORNER

Key Roles

Make sure the business has systems in place to allow for others to step into key roles in these situations. Critical systems would include:

- Ordering of materials
- Financials (making deposits, paying bills, billing customers)
- Plan for the "what if" situation and at least get the basics in order. It doesn't do you or the business any good to have to deal with a second crisis due to lack of planning after the immediate crisis is over.
- Determine a communication process for employees, customers, vendors and all key relationships.
- Have savings available to cover cash flow shortages incurred by the business disruption.
- Have key person insurance on critical people within the business.
- Know who you would call among your friends and trusted advisors and how they can help through the situation.

Financial Viability

As earlier chapters have addressed, the business must be financially viable, you must regularly review financial statements (and that means at least monthly, not just yearly) and you must understand your profitability on a regular basis.

As a side note, one of the first discussions I have with all my clients is about profitability. Do they really understand whether they are profitable and, if so, how profitable? The answer too often (in all sizes of companies) is that yes, they are profitable. Then I ask, "Do you pay yourself?" The answer is usually no. My answer then is, "No, you aren't profitable." If you aren't paying yourself a regular wage every payday, you need to take a wage and then take a look at profitability. This can be different during a startup phase, but that phase does not include your fifth year of being in business. The startup phase is more like the first one to two years.

A common scenario in family-owned businesses is for one of the owners to take home money as needed to cover the family living expenses. The other spouse (which unfortunately is often the wife) also works in the business but takes home no salary. Some may say, "So what; the family's living expenses are being covered." Yes, they are—at least for now. But what about longer term? No money is being put away to save for the potential that the spouse who is being paid is not in the picture (death, divorce). No retirement savings is being considered for either individual. Biblically the two become one in marriage, but that does not change the fact that each is an individual and each needs to ensure that anything that may happen in the future is taken into consideration.

One other thing to keep in mind is the mental and emotional toll that working for no pay creates. I have seen many situations where one spouse (again, it is usually the wife) is working—often full time—but because no actual money is in her name, her sense of value starts eroding. It may take some time, but after a few years, working for nothing will have a negative effect on even the strongest person. Also, if the business (after a startup time period) cannot support the people working in it, there are serious issues with the business.

Here's another way to look at this: If one business owner doesn't value the work of the spouse/other business owner, then why should the employees or the customers value them? By discounting the value of the spouse, most likely you are discounting the product or service you are offering, which essentially creates a spiral effect—and that isn't an upward spiral.

As we look at financial viability, there is another perspective to consider. How much of your family's and extended families' financial stability do you want to risk on the business?

I have heard of families with eight to 10 family members in the business (parents, siblings, in-laws). Now if this is a $50 million per year business that is run like a business and has an outside board of directors, that is a different type of risk that I am not covering in this book as there are many others that address those types of businesses. I am referring to the $1 million to $10 million business ventures with 10 to 50 employees where a large portion of the family is involved in the business. It can and has worked, but please make sure these considerations are being taken:

- **Disaster**—What if something happens to the business and there are no family members to fall back on as they are consumed by a crisis?
- **Economics**—When the business is not growing as desired (and trust me, this happens to all businesses at some point), how do you determine who takes a pay cut, doesn't get paid or is let go. The worst thing is not firing that family member who should go. If that employee weren't family, you probably wouldn't think twice. Yet the health of the business relies on your ability to think straight and run a business, not a family day care, meaning you take care of family members to the detriment of the business. To some that sounds harsh, yet you again have a choice—the health of the business and long-term success or failure that will take down everyone in the family. I have not yet heard of family business failures with large numbers of extended family members involved where the end result was good. It usually creates family rifts at a minimum and even lawsuits and families being torn apart permanently. This is discussed further in Chapter 12.
- **Checks and balances**—Yes, even in family businesses you *must* have checks and balances throughout the business. So what does that mean? At a minimum, have an outside CPA/accountant review the books on a regular basis for any inconsistencies. Ideally, whoever pays the bills doesn't do the bank reconciliation. Another individual looks at the financial statements monthly (if not more

often) and understands the accounts receivable (money collected and to be collected from customers) and accounts payable (what is owed to vendors). Talk to a CPA to figure out the best system of checks and balances for your business.

As was mentioned in the introduction all was going well in the business with the two brothers for a number of years until they found out the brother had been stealing money from the company for gambling and other things. It put the business and the family into bankruptcy, the family lost their house and the relationship with the brother has essentially never been repaired—and that was more than 20 years ago. There was enough blame and denial to fill another book, but the saddest part was all that is missed within the family. Nieces and nephews never get to know each other, family members die without relationships being repaired, the extended family doesn't gather for holidays.

These checks and balances structures must be set up at the beginning and validated on a regular basis so you don't wind up in this type of position. Use the philosophy "Trust, but verify." Trust your family members and employees, but verify and validate as a part of the business environment in order to minimize your chances of regret.

Let's talk about revenue and growth within a family business. Is this a lifestyle business, which means that you are working to make a good living? That also means you are putting aside money every year for retirement and using debt in a good way (not credit card debt) by leveraging the debt for growth. However, you may not be interested in double-digit growth or selling the business any time soon, and your work week is not at a harried pace that exhausts you or your family. If that is the case, then relax—that is fine. Not everyone has to set the world on fire with business growth. Now that may sound like heresy coming from a business coach, but this is your business and if you are making a good living and saving for retirement, then more power to you.

However, if you aren't making a good living (and make sure someone has challenged you as to what a good living is—it doesn't mean just getting by), you don't have retirement accounts or college funds, profit isn't where it should be, and your amount of debt keeps you up at night, then drastic changes to the business must take place.

CHAPTER 5

Finding the Balance Between Work and Play

Each of us has a spiritual aspect of our lives. It is what makes us whole. My spiritual foundation is in the Bible and has been my entire life. Why is the spiritual aspect important to the family business? We have five areas to our life: health, family, friends, spirituality and business.

Let's first look at business. No matter what, work will always be there. Being a business owner means that no matter how much you do, there will always be more. That is part of what drives business owners— the challenge to improve, the challenge to accomplish greater things, the challenge to try new things. However, without the other four areas (health, family, friends and spiritual life), we don't have balance. Balance is what makes it all worthwhile No matter how much we work, there will always be work to do; it's sort of like a bouncing ball—you bounce it and it bounces back to you. You might not even touch it and the ball continues to bounce. Yet if we ignore our health, it doesn't bounce back as easily (especially as we get older). If we ignore our friends, they stop calling and move on to someone else who does want to spend time with them. Ignore your marriage (even if you work with your spouse) and the end results can be devastating. Ignore your kids and they will find someone else who will care for them and spend time with them, and you might not like who it is.

We also have a spiritual aspect to who we are. For me, it is a relationship with God. For others, it is a different spiritual relationship or belief system. The result of ignoring that aspect of our lives is no different from ignoring family, friends or health.

Family business owners want balance. Balance reminds me visually of the scales of justice that are perfectly balanced. In reality, especially for a family business owner, balance is not something to strive for as the result will leave you highly frustrated. Harmony is more of the concept you should consider. Think of a vocal music presentation: Sometimes the altos stand out, sometimes the sopranos, but overall the vocal parts all meld together as one cohesive orchestra

When you own a business, sometimes the business must be your priority. Sometimes the priority is home or friends or health. The reality is to understand there must be harmony between them. One month you have tremendous deadlines, new business, growth and challenges within the business, so you need to put in 14-hour days. That cannot continue for years or it will affect the business. However, the next week there are soccer games, date night and a weekend away so the pressures of work must remain at work.

It is all about choices and the choices are for *you* to make; don't let others make those choices for you. We have all heard music in which the harmony is out of balance and it isn't pleasant to the ear or to life.

Perspectives on Abundance

What is your attitude toward money? Does your mindset need to change? Are you afraid of making money, or lots of money? Before you laugh and say no, it is very common. Contrary to popular belief, probably

80 percent of those who own small family businesses need to work on their attitude toward money. They don't feel they need much, yet they don't have any idea how they will pay for retirement, they have debt, and they don't really know how much it takes them to live each year or where they spend their money.

Money is a tool to be used for the benefit of you and others. However, as 1 Timothy 6:10 says, "For the love of money is a root of all kinds of evil." In addition to the obvious interpretation that the pursuit of financial gain is evil, some people develop a belief that they are only worth a particular dollar amount. No less, but no more. As a result, they often undervalue themselves and their products. That includes not making enough money in your business to create market value and growth within the business. Just getting by is no less an evil than making millions and being a miser or allowing it to be a god to you. Too many lottery winners end up broke, miserable, friendless and unhappy. Most of it stems not from having the money but not understanding the tool and how to utilize the tool.

> *Family businesses often undervalue themselves and their products, including not making enough money to create market value and growth within the business.*

Let's translate this to profit. Do you believe you should be profitable? If so, how much is too much? Kyle owned a small business with his wife, Kim. They had owned it for almost 25 years and loved the reputation they had in town. Everyone knew that if you wanted something printed you should go to their business because they were really inexpensive. That was wonderful for their customers. However, truth be told, Kyle and Kim had almost no savings, their house had a large mortgage and they had debts on the business. Their ability to retire or even respond to a personal emergency was minimal. Should something happen to one of them, the business would most likely go bankrupt since they had no cushion to get them through an unforeseen circumstance. Most everyone had told them to raise their prices, but fear of being perceived as greedy consumed them and they never did.

How would a 10 percent price increase affect their profit? It would increase it 10 percent. Let's look at an example. Let's say their business had about $300,000 in revenue with a 5 percent profit, which is $15,000 per year. Increasing their prices by 10 percent would increase their revenue by $30,000 to $330,000. There would not be any additional cost for increasing their prices and it would net them an additional $30,000 in profit. What impact would $30,000 have in this situation? It would make a huge difference in their savings, quality of life and rainy day fund should that unforeseen circumstance arise.

If you don't have a healthy perspective on money as a tool and a mindset of abundance, it will be reflected in the profits for your business, your quality of life and your ability to achieve your dreams.

Luke 16 (NIV) relates a parable Jesus is telling his disciples about a rich man whose manager was accused of wasting his possessions. As the owner of a family business, are you wasting what has been given to you? "There was a rich man whose manager was accused of wasting his possessions. So he called him in and asked him, 'What is this I hear about you? Give an account of your management.'" (Luke 16:1–2) Through either mismanagement or fraud, the business had lost serious money. The manager knew that the books would reveal his role in the losses, and his heart sank.

You may or may not like to hear this, but Jesus is telling this story to encourage you to see yourself as a manager, not an owner. All your stuff is really God's, and he seems to think that you are accountable to him for the way in which you accumulate it and spend it. Is he lord of your checkbook? Your portfolio? Your real estate? If he audited you today to analyze how you are managing his property, would you be proud or terrified?

Women in Business

As far back as the Old Testament we see women in business. Yet there is still often a perspective that women don't belong in the business world.

That is changing, but it hasn't been that many years ago that it was very difficult for women to get loans, buy businesses and be the business owner.

Proverbs 31:10–31 (NIV) is the story of the Wife of Noble Character. Verses 16–18 say: "She considers a field and buys it; out of her earnings she plants a vineyard. She sets about her work vigorously; her arms are strong for her tasks. She sees that her trading is profitable, and her lamp does not go out at night."

This paints a picture of the woman business owner thousands of years ago who bought and sold in the process of running her business. She earned money and created a profit. Notice the verse says she was profitable. That is the purpose of a business—to earn a profit. Often our beliefs regarding money condition our mindset about money. So many people don't believe they deserve to make money or very much money.

One of my friends had his daughter read the book *Think and Grow Rich* by Napoleon Hill, which is a fantastic book and one I recommend every business owner read. After his daughter (who was 13 at the time) finished the book, she commented that it was OK, but all it focused on was money. She wanted to help people. There are many ways to

> *That is the purpose of a business—to earn a profit.*

help people, and each of us must determine our passion and how we want to help others. It is our responsibility to use those gifts in the best way possible. Often that gift is to make money through our businesses to help others. Money is a requirement of society. Those who have it have the opportunity to give to others so they can continue their work. My challenge to my friend's daughter is if you have been given the gift to be able to earn money, then it is your responsibility to earn it, give it away and therefore help others.

Let's continue with verses 20–21: "She opens her arms to the poor and extends her hands to the needy. When it snows, she has no fear for her household; for all of them are clothed in scarlet."

Scarlet clothing in Old Testament times was considered a luxury. To wear scarlet (including her children and servants; notice it says "household") meant the fruits of the woman's labor were substantial.

How does this relate to a family business in today's society? Too often I see the family structure within the business not respecting the role of the women who work for the business. Their ability to run, manage and operate the business is often greater than the other family members, but they do not receive proper recognition. The successful family business really looks at each family member as being equal and utilizes those gifts accordingly.

More and more I see the husband in the family turn over the role of "president" to the wife. He may have the product expertise, but it takes more than product expertise to run a business. More than one business I have worked with has done that exact thing. The husband has not enjoyed the operational management aspect of the business. He enjoys sales or product delivery or research. Managing, motivating, creating vision, or just being president is best accomplished by the wife in this situation.

> *The successful family business really looks at each family member as being equal and utilizes those gifts accordingly.*

The danger within the family is giving the wife (or husband, as this role can be reversed as well) the role when she isn't qualified to take on the responsibilities or doesn't want to. Tom had been running the business for a number of years. As it grew and he encountered challenges, they decided to bring his wife into the business. Susan really didn't have a heart for the business, but did it because they had heard that women-owned businesses received priority for certain types of business within their community, especially government work. So they decided to name her president. (As a note: Because she really didn't know much about the product they offered and she only worked in the business about 15 hours per week, their company didn't qualify as a woman-owned business, so naming her president never did get them any additional business.) She didn't understand the business and what it took to make decisions, and Tom started blaming his inability to make decisions on Susan. After a few years, everyone who dealt with them knew that Susan was president in name only and that Tom was making poor business decisions, and as a result they lost business and credibility.

COACH'S CORNER

Be A Leader

If you are going to be in business, then be in the business. Don't hide behind a title and don't take one just to circumvent a policy. If you are going to be the president, then be the president and work on the business. Be the leader.

Here are a few recommendations for women business owners:

+ Don't listen to anyone who tells you that you won't succeed. That is their opinion and one that you don't share. Find books about women who have succeeded against all odds. Mary Kate Ash, the founder of Mary Kay, is a good example. She was told her business would never work and she should quit. Her husband died as they were starting the business and the bank refused to provide her the funding she needed. She had determination and a plan and she executed it. There were challenges, but they helped her focus on what she needed to accomplish.

+ Make sure you have a support team around you of both men and women who believe in what you are doing and where you are going.

+ Take care of yourself. Neglecting your health doesn't help you succeed.

+ You can be Wonder Woman. But do you want to? Years ago I had the full-time career, nanny at home with my son, outside volunteer activities, a vacation home. Then I decided that while I could have it all, I just didn't really want it all. I wanted time with my family and that is the legacy that lives on. I didn't give up the career, but I did refocus my spare time. In the long run, I created a higher level of success just by refocusing my energies.

+ Take charge of situations. Others may want to walk all over you if you let them. Don't let them.
+ Have confidence, especially when you don't.
+ Failure is a process, not an event. Learn from everything that doesn't go the right way, apply it and know that failure just takes you one step closer to where you want to be.

"Never, never, never give up." —WINSTON CHURCHILL

PART TWO

Motivation for Having a Family Business

For some, the American dream means owning your own business. There are many reasons for this dream. Money, job security, the dislike of working for someone else, opportunities in the marketplace, desire for control, and lack of opportunities elsewhere are just some of the reasons. Regardless of the underlying reason, the drive can be powerful for the family that dreams of working together.

Yet it is often those very reasons that can get the family business into trouble both in the business and in the family.

CHAPTER 6

Mindset

Before we look at the motivations of a family business, the critical aspect of *mindset* must be addressed. What does mindset have to do with getting into a family business, being successful or working with your family? **EVERYTHING.**

Why are you in business? Read Simon Sinek's *Start With Why* or go to YouTube for Simon's TED video, http://youtu.be/qp0HIF3SfI4. Every business owner must understand WHY they are in business before they work through the WHAT and HOW of the business. Yet, knowing WHY you are in business must be balanced with the correct mindset. A mindset of:

+ Abundance, not scarcity
+ Results, not excuses
+ Ownership, not denial
+ Accountability, not blame

Below are a few questions for consideration:

+ How do you handle failure?
+ What is your perspective of failure?
+ When you fail, how long does it take you to pick yourself up?
+ What happens to your composure when something goes wrong?
+ Do you blame others for things that happen, or do you look to yourself for ownership?
+ Are you quick to forgive, or do you hold grudges?
+ Where does your self-esteem come from?
+ How do you perceive the failure of others?
+ What do you do when you are told no?

In his book *Failing Forward*, John Maxwell talks about what failing is not.

Failing is not:

1. **Avoidable**—Each of us is human; we fail, and we fail on a regular basis. Failure becomes a stumbling block when we don't learn from our failures and continue making the same mistakes time after time after time. Darren Hardy, the editor of *Success* magazine, actually talks about setting a failure quota each day. You aren't pushing yourself if you aren't failing at something. That's a very different perspective, isn't it! For you to have a successful family business, everyone in the family must begin to understand and accept the concept of failure and move past holding failures over others' heads. Fail, pick yourself up, learn, move forward and keep on going.

2. **An Event**—Think back to when you were in high school (even though it may have been a while for some of us). If we failed to pass a test, the failure didn't come on the day of the test. The failure probably started the first day of class and continued when we failed to pay attention, take the teacher seriously, take notes,

do the homework, study as we went along and ask for help when we didn't understand. The test was only a snapshot of what had been happening all along. That is true in your business as well. If revenue is down for the year, the end of the year is not the time to start a marketing campaign that needed to start 12 months ago. If you lose a client, you didn't lose the client the day she quit ordering from you; you lost her months ago by not having the systems in place to know what was truly going on with her.

3. **Objective**—What determines whether an action is a failure is all in the mind of the individual. Read Walter Isaacson's biography of Steve Jobs. Steve failed multiple times; in fact, he once got fired from his own company. It was that failure that forced him to do new things like create Pixar, which laid the groundwork for where Apple was when Steve Jobs passed away. If we look at individual events as failures, we will never pick ourselves up to move on.

4. **The Enemy**—Do you remember every success you have ever had? Do you remember your failures? We learn far more from our failures than we do our successes. We analyze failure; we seldom analyze success. Learn to embrace the failure, and your growth will become exponential.

5. **Irreversible**—Steve Jobs got fired from Apple. He later went back to Apple and made it a great company. Stop looking at today's failure as being irreversible and something that can't be changed. It is a state of mind for today and today only. Move on.

6. **A Stigma**—A great baseball player could bat .333. That means he gets about one hit every three times he's at bat. Does that stop him from trying to hit another ball? NO! If it did, he would never have made it to the pros. He knows he must shake off the misses and keep on swinging.

7. **Final**—The only thing that is final is death. Everything else needs time and perspective. Give your failure time and you can change your perspective of a failure into a mindset of learning and opportunity.

Keep these points in mind while we take a look at a few of the primary drivers for owning a family business in the next several chapters.

CHAPTER 7

Control

Control freak" is often an apt description of business owners. We like the ability to control our destiny, make our own decisions and see the impact of what we accomplish. The challenge comes with:

+ Understanding how little control we actually have; it's really just a perception of control.
+ Learning how to relinquish control, i.e., delegate, for the business to grow.
+ Leveraging our controlling nature into something successful.

The Dream

Sal kept watching how the business was run, the waste that was taking place, how customers were being treated and the lack of profit that was being generated. These frustrations led to his determination to start his own business. Sal's premise was that he would treat employees much better than his current employer did, eliminate waste, treat his customers better and generate more profit. In essence, Sal wanted control over the areas in which his current employer struggled. He accomplished those goals. He also learned a number of lessons in the process.

These goals were Sal's primary drivers for family business ownership (and possibly entrepreneurship in general). The person who wants to start a business:

+ Is tired of following someone else's lead/orders
+ Believes they can serve the customer better
+ Has different ideas on how to implement the product or service
+ Desires flexibility in their day-to-day lives and a better balance between work and home
+ Craves the ability to make more money

The lessons these new business owners learn are:

+ Their new boss (themselves and their family) is not the wonderful boss they thought they would be and they have a great deal to learn. The new boss in the mirror isn't always a pretty sight. They find that the new boss is demanding, doesn't give vacations, doesn't allow employees to sleep in, has become more of a perfectionist, is always striving to improve and the list goes on. The situation is reminiscent of the age-old statement "The grass is always greener on the other side of the fence."
+ They can serve the customer better, but it is much harder than they thought and they start to understand their old company better. Customers can be and often are demanding. Their interpretation of quality is different from yours. You may see value in something that the customer doesn't care about.
+ They have different ideas on implementation; some of those ideas work and some don't.
+ Flexibility is fantastic—you can work any part of the 24 hours per day that you want. Yes, you do have flexibility to take your kids to school, pick them up, go to their activities, etc., but there is a cost,

and that cost is often working evenings and weekends and other times that you didn't have to work at your previous job.

The Reality

The more we want and think we have control, the less we have. There is always someone else who truly has more control. It might be customers, the government, laws, acts of God. It is that desire for control that if not managed well drains the business. The inability to delegate is the result of the business owner's desire to have control. They can do it better than anyone else. They serve the clients better, they know the product better, and there-fore they don't delegate. They truly want the control and the ego boost that comes with it. Stop it *now*. Learn how to delegate.

> *The new boss in the mirror isn't always a pretty sight.*

Suzie had been a controlling person for years. She worked long hours and had a high standard for how things got done. After years of working like this, her energy level and her love of the business began to deteriorate. After being coached for a while, she began to realize that others could probably do things as well as she could or, more importantly, better. Slowly she began to document how to do tasks that she had always thought only she should do. She realized that one of her office team members could enter some of the bills and that she was actually faster than Suzie. That freed up some time to work on more strategic activities. The end result was business growth, increased profit and a happier office team since they were now more empowered and felt more valued.

After you have determined the above and decided who should com-plete the task, do the following:

+ Review the task to be delegated, and make sure the employee knows and understands what needs to be done. (See chapter 13 for further details on behavior assessments.) Let them own the task.

COACH'S CORNER

The Steps to Delegating

The following process can help you begin to delegate.

Determine:

- The value of your time. (See chapter 2 for details on this process.) This will help you determine which of your tasks you need to give up.

- What you like to do the least. Often I see owners who like to do everything, so making this list is more difficult.

- How to document what it is you do. Essentially this is creating a system so what you are delegating is accomplished the way you want it done. I have attempted to document everything I do that can be delegated, even to standard responses to emails. If I have had to write essentially the same email more than once, then I stop, think about what message I want to convey, write a template version and then save it in a place where I can find it easily. I may need to edit the template for the specific situation, but I don't have to start the thinking from scratch and then forget an important point. I just make sure I read the email before I send it so it makes sense with my edits. It may save me only a minute, but minutes count.

- Who has the best attitude to accomplish the task you want to delegate. Notice that I didn't start with skill set. Attitude is far more important than skill set.

- Who has the necessary skill set to accomplish the task or whether the task is trainable. Almost anything is trainable. The assumption is that if you need to delegate an engineering task, you have qualified engineers on the team who can accomplish the tasks. If not, then you have a completely different issue at hand.

- Follow up. This is about delegation, not abdication. Too often those who don't like to delegate have tried what they thought was delegation, but what they really did was abdicate the responsibility.

Abdication is handing over the task and walking away, never to check up, follow up or validate that the task is being done, let alone being done well. Delegation means you check in, ask good questions, and ensure the project is on target for completion and will be accomplished as you desire.

Now, go start this process all over again with another area that you should be delegating!

This process may take a few attempts to ensure you are doing it well, but the end result is that you no longer need to do that task. Someone else can do it and you can leverage yourself, your time and your business to accomplish even greater things.

Learning to Let Go

Teach your team how to accomplish tasks better than you. An indication that the owner wants control is customers wanting to deal only with the owner. The owners fear is that no one can do it as well as he can. So he or she does everything. Reality is others can do many to most of the tasks as well or better than you. However, it is important to provide training, education and most especially the authority to act and to resolve customer issues. Hearing "My customers only want to deal with me" is quite common but is also very preventable and can be addressed.

Many of these issues are due to the lack of systems within the business and the owner's desire for control. Remember, one of the reasons the business was started was to gain control. That desire to control is now beginning to hurt the business and, just as importantly, preventing growth and increased profitability. Most importantly, you need to allow non-family members to be a part of the family, resolve problems, create solutions and therefore create value in the business you are working at so hard. How do you solve the situation? Here is an example:

Everyone wanted to deal only with Sam. He was the owner and was the best at delivering the services of his business, and everyone knew it. When he received referrals, everyone said, "Ask for Sam. You will get more value for their product (oh, and by the way, he will give you a discount if you ask)." Now Sam knew this, but he didn't know how to stop discounting and start turning the customer interaction over to his son, Jim. His son was getting frustrated because everyone wanted Dad and often Dad overrode Jim when he gave the price to a customer. Jim was getting ready to give up and start being just like Dad— discounting and overdelivering the service. Now that may sound good if you are the customer, but the business was bleeding cash. There wasn't enough of it at the end of the month. Dad was burned out and ready to throw in the towel on the business.

What happened next revolutionized the business and the family relationships. Sam started taking Jim with him on all his service calls. Sam really trained Jim how to deal with customers (both the good and the not quite so good). Sam then shared with his customers how he was changing how he did business and that Sam was getting out of the field to focus on the business itself so they could grow and improve how they were servicing their customers. Jim would now be the primary technician and Sam had all the confidence in the world that Jim would do an even better job than Sam had ever done. With this change, they also created a price list that would be used for all customers. A couple of other changes also took place: Sam started talking up Jim with his clients. He would continually mention how good Jim was and how Jim was actually better than Sam. Two things happened: Jim actually started getting better than Sam and Jim's confidence in his ability increased even more as customers started preferring Jim to Sam.

The hard part in this type of environment is letting go of the control and your ego (yes, much of it is ego) and taking those first steps to let someone else actually be better at delivering the product and service. It is often one of the hardest things a business owner must do, but it must happen. It is also about attitude. If you truly believe that no one else can do a task as well as you, then you will never give anyone the opportunity. However, I will say that there is always someone who can deliver to the customer at least as well as, if not better than, you, but you must find that person, invest in them and have the commitment to make it happen.

Within a few months, Jim was having fun, profit had gone up and Sam was enjoying his new role as a business owner, not the technician. Customers were now asking for Jim and not Sam, which excited Sam even more, What Sam did in the process of turning things over to Jim in the field was:

+ He trained Jim in the way of the business.
+ He passed along confidence and authority to his new technician, Jim. (This works with non-family members as well.)
+ He had created systems for how to do things that Jim could follow and also documented why the system was important to follow. Most people will resist when they are told to do something in a certain way and they don't really want to. However, if you put a system together for doing something as simple as answering the phone and help the person responsible to better understand how that simple act of answering the phone impacts profitability, then you create a sense of pride, ownership and contribution. If *you* don't know why answering the phone impacts profitability, then another discussion is required.
+ He empowered Jim to stick to the price list. Sam had a hard time holding to a price list and not discounting, but Jim had no problem with it. This was the price and that was that.

Some of you are probably scared to death by this process and worry about losing customers. After all, price is the one reason that people do business with you. Right? Wrong. The reality is that you are losing money by discounting since the discount is your profit. Go back to chapter 2 and figure out who your ideal client or target customer is and focus on them. If the shoppers who are focused solely on price leave, their complaints will follow them and your profit will increase. See table 1 for a chart that shows how discounting affects your profitability and then see table 2 for how price increases also affect profitability.

Discounting Your Prices

If Your Present Margin Is ...

by:	20%	25%	30%	35%	40%	45%	50%	55%	60%
	Your sales must INCREASE by the amount shown below to keep the *same* margin								
2%	11%	9%	7%	6%	5%	5%	4%	4%	3%
4%	25%	19%	15%	13%	11%	10%	9%	8%	7%
6%	43%	32%	25%	21%	18%	15%	14%	12%	11%
8%	67%	47%	36%	30%	25%	22%	19%	17%	15%
10%	100%	67%	50%	40%	33%	29%	25%	22%	20%
12%	150%	92%	67%	52%	43%	36%	32%	28%	25%
14%	233%	127%	88%	67%	54%	45%	39%	34%	30%
16%	400%	178%	114%	84%	67%	55%	47%	41%	36%
18%	900%	257%	150%	106%	82%	67%	56%	49%	43%
20%	–	400%	200%	133%	100%	80%	67%	57%	50%
25%	–	–	500%	250%	167%	125%	100%	83%	71%
30%	–	–	–	600%	300%	200%	150%	120%	100%

And you *discount* your price

Table 1

Table 1 indicates the *increase* in your sales required to compensate for a price discounting strategy. For example, if your margin is 40 percent and you reduce your price by 10 percent, you would need your sales volume to increase by 33 percent to maintain your profit. Rarely has such a strategy worked in the past and it's unlikely it will work in the future!

Increasing Your Prices

If Your Present Margin Is ...

	20%	25%	30%	35%	40%	45%	50%	55%	60%
And you increase your price									
by:	Your sales would have to DECLINE by the amount shown before your profit is reduced								
2%	9%	7%	6%	5%	5%	4%	4%	4%	3%
4%	17%	14%	12%	10%	9%	8%	7%	7%	6%
6%	23%	19%	17%	15%	13%	12%	11%	10%	9%
8%	29%	24%	21%	19%	17%	15%	14%	13%	12%
10%	33%	29%	25%	22%	20%	18%	17%	15%	14%
12%	38%	32%	29%	26%	23%	21%	19%	18%	17%
14%	41%	36%	32%	29%	26%	24%	22%	20%	19%
16%	44%	39%	35%	31%	29%	26%	24%	23%	21%
18%	47%	42%	38%	34%	31%	29%	26%	25%	23%
20%	50%	44%	40%	36%	33%	31%	29%	27%	25%
25%	56%	50%	45%	42%	38%	36%	33%	31%	29%
30%	60%	55%	50%	46%	43%	40%	38%	35%	33%

Table 2

When you adopt a premium pricing strategy, table 2 shows the amount by which your sales would have to decline following a price increase *before* your gross profit is reduced below its current level. For example, at the same 40 percent margin, a 10 percent increase in your price could sustain a 20 percent reduction in sales volume.

COACH'S CORNER

Letting Go

+ Understand that you sacrifice one level of control for another. When you work for someone else, they have control over what you do, when you do it, how you do it and, for that matter, if you do it. Having your own business doesn't necessarily mean you have control. Other things control you: customers, finances, regulations, economic situations, life changes. It is all about understanding what you give up and what you get and having an attitude that helps you overcome the challenges. Planning is absolutely critical and provides you the control that you truly desire. Yet 80 percent of family business owners fail to plan and so they do not have the control they sought.

+ Never stop learning: Always be reading, listening, attending conferences or meeting with other business owners—especially family business owners—to learn what they do, how to improve your own skill set and how to keep your personal growth moving forward.

+ Always ask questions. Questions can make the difference between success and greater success. The good decision and a great decision. Learn the art of asking questions and not telling.

CHAPTER **8**

Passion for a
Product or Service

A skill creates an opportunity; a love for a service creates a business; a vision becomes a product that will change the lives of others. All of these can be the foundation for a new business. Many times this passion creates a momentum that the creators haven't even dreamed of. Their vision snowballs into a business beyond their wildest imagination.

At times this passion comes with years of education like the medical or dental fields, engineering or many other degreed trades. To quote a client:

"Practicing dentistry since 1993, I never thought of myself as a business owner. I preferred to go to the office, do my dentistry and then call it a day. Needless to say, my lack of business sense eventually caught up with me. A realization hit me that I needed to look at my dental practice as a business, not just a place to do dentistry."

He was coached and now has an amazing practice with an amazing staff. His revenue and profit increased that first year of coaching and he is now a business owner as well as a fantastic dentist. His wife and sister-in-law work in the business as well, making it a truly family-owned business. He is continued what is now three centuries of dental practice in his family. That is a long time.

Yes, it is a business, yet so often the doctor, dentist or lawyer thinks of themselves first as a doctor, dentist or lawyer. They have a passion for their trade, but don't consider themselves a business owner. As a result, the business, clients and employees often suffer. Business is up and down, and employees aren't really managed well. ("After all," the professional thinks, "I am a doctor, not a manager.")

They entered into their profession because of their love of medicine or the law, or they wanted to help people, but it is that passion that often actually gets in the way of delivering the quality they envisioned.

A father came home from the war with a passion for flying and founded a business that allowed him to live his passion. Fifty years later, his sons, the business founders, brothers and grandchildren are working at the business. The challenge comes from the reality that family-owned businesses often implode by the third or fourth generation. So how do you leave the legacy to the family with a level of comfort that the family will not be torn apart in a future generation? One option is to consider merging before it becomes a necessity. Often the second and third generations aren't the visionaries and drivers to get the business to the next level of success.

Facing the Challenges

The challenge that the older generation has is developing true leadership in subsequent generations. The kids may know the family business, but they may not know business, which is very different from knowing the basic products and services that started the company. So when being purchased or merging become options, the family members are essentially unprepared for what the future may hold. That protectionist nature that prevails in the older generations can really haunt the future.

It comes back to denial—denial that the founder will die, denial that changes are inevitable.

Another challenge is when the older generation doesn't want to let go. Fear stands in their way of letting the new leadership actually take risks, try new things and emerge as leaders. Parents don't always make the transition of seeing their kids as adults, ready to make adult decisions for the business—and this can take place even when the "kids" are in their 40s or 50s.

Patronage is another challenge created by family dynasties. This prevents the rest of the employees from rising in the ranks of the business and stifles honest feedback to the owners and other family members.

What are solutions for these situations?

Run the business like a business. This means you need to be objective, have a business plan and make sure there is an organization chart for where the business is now and where you want the business to be in five years. Make decisions not on emotion, but on sound business practices. Have a better understanding of where your emotions get in your way; this is the subjective part of how you run the business rather than the objective side. Ensure all family members continue to be educated in the business. Make sure they attend education workshops outside of your industry on a regular basis. They

> *Make decisions not on emotion, but on sound business practices.*

need to read or listen to CDs about topics in which they need to expand their knowledge. Have a process and level of accountability that demands outside learning. This should be viewed not as an investment in the business but as an investment in the individual. To quote Jim Rohn: "Don't wish things were easier, wish that you were better." Invest in yourself on a regular basis and you will never regret it.

Learn to let go. The current owners must sit down with the next generation of leadership and determine rules of the game. These rules must allow for growth, failure, opportunities and learning. You as the current business owners made mistakes. You as the current business owners starting this transition must allow the next generation to make their own mistakes. The ideas will be different, new, foreign and sometimes scary. Without you letting go—just like you did when those children learned how to walk—they won't be ready to take on the challenges of the business when you are gone. Let the next generation learn with your expert guidance and the ability to ask questions without passing judgment of why something won't work or what could go wrong.

Understand the effect of patronage. Patronage is the custom of filling positions with people you want in the position, no matter what their qualifications and experience. Patronage is alive and well in all family-owned businesses. On the positive side, patronage is what creates the family business. It automatically creates a sense of loyalty and rewards those who are a part of it. On the other hand, patronage creates a one-sided organization with one viewpoint and a blind eye to opposing views. Patronage allows for those who are not competent to hold a position for which they are not qualified. This affects the business's effort to build value that should be a part of the business culture. It allows for waste and special behavior that is contradictory to the goals of the business.

Patronage can have its positives; it allows the ability to employ, train and utilize family members, close friends and relatives who need a break that doesn't seem to come their way for one reason or another. It can be the opportunity that allows them to succeed, create a positive self-image and become a productive member of society.

Tom had a close friend and neighbor, Bill, who had a tremendous gift for working with his hands in building and carpentry. Throughout high school and his late teens, Bill had abused drugs and alcohol. As a result, his discipline and normal business functioning skills—like showing up for work on time—were lacking. Yet Tom saw the potential in Bill and offered him a job. Bill worked with Tom for a number of years. Yes, there were concessions, there was teaching and there were times for holding him accountable. Bill learned from that process. Tom learned to keep business and personal separate. He would hold Bill accountable for quality of work, showing up on time, dressing appropriately when interacting with customers and so on. Outside of work they could be friends, socialize and enjoy each other's company. Bill actually grew up, determined what he wanted to do with his life and was able to move on, armed with great potential. This is patronage at its best. The job would not have been offered if there had not been an upfront relationship and therefore an opportunity.

Patronage at its worst comes in the form of hiring a person and then having to deal with a total lack of accountability and productivity. George was the son of the owner. He lacked social skills, attention to detail and common business sense. However, George was employed in a fairly critical role in the company, handling its IT functions. He was skilled at IT, but about every three weeks he would not show up for a week. The staff needed the expertise, there wasn't a backup person and George not showing up affected their ability to service customers. Unfortunately the owner would not hear of making any changes, providing any additional support or getting George the help he needed. The result was a culture of excuses within the company. No one was held accountable and the company muddled along instead of growing.

What is the solution to this type of problem? I understand it is hard, but it is solvable as long as someone is willing to face the reality. In this case, George and the company needed help. If not having George work in the company was not an option, they could have created a work environment in which someone was able to help when George was not available. That could be another employee or an outside service as a backup. The arrangement could have been presented in a kind, compassionate way to the whole team: "This is how it works with George. We as a company have compassion for those who potentially cannot hold down a full-time job 40 hours per week 52 weeks per year. However, for those of us who can, here are the standards. Here is what we expect and excuses are not an option."

There are times when patronage is appropriate. There is a wonderful deli down the street from me that has great food and a fun atmosphere. One of the employees there has Down syndrome and works to clean up around the deli. He does great work, but is a bit loud at times and a bit disruptive occasionally. Those who work there know how to handle him, calm him down and focus his efforts. All of us who frequent the deli know and understand the environment and that this worker is a vital part of that establishment. If people are uncomfortable, they can eat elsewhere. Those are different circumstances and not really at play when we discuss patronage.

CHAPTER 9

Buying a Job

The recession that began in 2007 created a high level of sustained unemployment for a large segment of the population. This has actually created a fairly large number of new business startups and, in some cases, business acquisitions for those who want to buy a job. Some have come to the realization that there isn't a job for them in the marketplace, while others have realized that for various reasons they don't want the jobs that are available. They need to continue making a living, so what are the other options? The concept of buying a job isn't wrong in any way, as long as they make the transition from being the employee to being the business owner. I often joke that they trade in the boss they didn't like when they worked for someone else for the really bad boss—the one who looks them in the mirror every morning. Often that old boss doesn't seem so bad after all.

When someone buys a job, it often becomes a family affair with kids, siblings and spouse becoming involved. All the standard opportunities and challenges apply. Don't run from the opportunity—but know what you are getting into. Here the lack of capitalization can be the difference between success and failure. The average business owner needs one to two years of capital (without the owner getting paid much or getting paid at all) to survive and then thrive. Without adequate capital, you essentially starve the business by needing to take out what is working capital to make it a success.

When you buy a job, you have often lost your income and aren't expecting to get another job for a long period of time. If you don't have another source of income to pay the bills, the squeeze begins occurring very quickly and being trapped in a vise starts looking more comfortable.

> *The reality is that buying a job can be quite fulfilling.*

The upside is being in control, being able to do what you love, having flexibility, leveraging your time and money, exercising creativity, enjoying freedom and experiencing all the other joys of business ownership. It is awesome. You will learn, grow, and see new challenges and opportunities, but be sure to do your research before you jump.

Buying a job really means taking something you know or want to know and buying into it. Franchises are often filled with people buying jobs. They have some money to invest and rather than getting a new job, they choose to buy a company or a franchise. Great money can be made here, and there is a fantastic opportunity to work with your spouse, yet you must run it like a business, not a hobby and not just a job.

The reality is that buying a job can be quite fulfilling. The ability to work alongside your spouse can be great fun. The ability to create, deliver and earn a living with someone who is many business owners' best friend—their spouse—is really a dream come true. It is fun to travel together, solve problems, challenge themselves, grow and reproduce. No, I don't mean reproduce from a biological perspective; what I mean is reproduce through team members and employees to create that work family situation that makes everyone want to come to work. Often the family business owner has the latitude to create a work environment that is the envy of those not a part of it.

That is one of the environments I had in the past. The work environment was challenging yet caring, growing yet balanced, fun yet with an eye toward priorities, profitable yet not at the expense of others. When that business was sold—so all of us as owners could reap the benefits and the primary stockholder could retire—there was sadness. The family was torn apart, and it wasn't ever the same. The business continues to this day, but the loss is felt by many who were a part of the family team that was created. That can be one of the joys of having a family business.

A success for me was helping a retired individual who wanted to manufacture a product he felt was needed. When he really did the research, including finding out the manufacturing costs, the necessary investment and the competition, he determined it would not achieve his goal. The fact that he chose not to invest his retirement savings on a product that would not provide a return on investment that he didn't have the time to recover from is what I consider a success. He came to that conclusion himself, not by me telling him. He walked away with the understanding that he had pursued his idea and decided it was not the right step; this allowed him to move on with dignity and no wasted money. We both now sleep well at night!

If you have started your own business to provide a job, congratulations. Now make it a good, profitable job that provides for your family and builds value for you and your community. The challenge goes back to that value proposition. A business broker was lamenting the challenge of helping those who bought jobs for themselves. They now want to sell that job. They built their company so it provides a paycheck—and sometimes even a reasonable paycheck. The other reality is that you can't sell a job!

If you have created a job in a family business, don't have the unrealistic expectation that you will be able to sell this job. If others want to create a job, they can do so for probably far less money than it will take to buy the job from you. However, if you started by buying a job and then created a business that has value, you have created a legacy from which you can leverage all your hard work. Decide early on which it is and try not to deceive yourself.

Here is the reality of buying a job and not turning it into a business: The meaning of the word JOB becomes Just Over Broke. You may buy a job, but turn it into a business—you will be forever grateful.

Table 3 points out some differences between a job and a business of value:

Job	Business
Generates a paycheck for the owner and family	Creates value and profitability
Is based on the owner's ability to generate revenue	Leverages the owner's knowledge but not the owner's labor to generate revenue and profit
Doesn't worry about business profitability, only the family paycheck	Understands profitability is the key to leveraging business growth and long-term value. Revenue is ego, profitability is reality and cash is king.
Adds value to the community through the individual only	Adds value to the community through the business
	Adds value to employees, suppliers and others

Table 3

CHAPTER **10**

Career Change

The second-career family business is fairly prevalent in certain types of business environments, including hobby businesses (which are addressed in chapter 11), bed and breakfasts, restaurants, retail outlets and outdoor type ventures, such as fishing expeditions. As most of us head into our 40s, 50s and even 60s, we begin to look at what we want to do with the next 20 or more years. Often the thought of doing the same thing we have been doing is overwhelming. I remember being in my late 30s and 40s thinking I didn't want to do my current job for the next 20 years. I enjoyed what I did, but the thought of staying there for two more decades made me feel almost claustrophobic. I stayed in the role I was in for a good decade more and enjoyed 95 percent of what I did. Yet that desire to branch out into new and uncharted territories from a career perspective really became strong the older I got.

For me I was pretty sure I didn't want to work full time with my husband. We had actually started our careers that way. We worked at the same place when we met and worked together for two years while dating and then got married. Due to a number of circumstances, we both left that employer within about two months of getting married. Yet without any planning, our new jobs ended up being at the same company. It worked well; we had fun and it was sometimes challenging, and I wouldn't change it for anything.

Actually as my role in the company grew, I ended up being one of the executives at the business. My husband, Steve, was implementing the software systems our company provided. One of our customers was not happy. The product we offered had been oversold by one of our new sales team, and the customer was taking it out on the implementation team, which my husband headed up. The call came in from that customer. I had never spoken to her before, but I was the executive she reached. She proceeded to take the next 15 minutes to tell me what a horrible job Steve had done and how she didn't like doing business with us among several other complaints. When I had taken her call, I knew she was upset and wanted her to feel comfortable being open about the issues. My desire was not to mislead her but to allow her to be open. I knew that sharing my last name would most likely shut down communication. So I introduced myself by title and first name. I truly didn't expect the diatribe out of her that I received. We talked through the issues and laid out a plan for resolution, and she settled down. She thanked me profusely for listening and said she really liked our plan.

She then asked for my name and title again. I said the same thing that I did upon introduction: "My name is Janna and I am the vice president, so I will get things done for you." She then asked for my last name. Now I was stuck; she had really unloaded about the person serving her—who happened to be my husband. I didn't want to embarrass her, make her uncomfortable or undo what we had just accomplished. Yet no matter how I tried to sidestep the question, she asked again for my last name. I told her, and was greeted with silence. She then said, "Are you any relation to Steve?" I wasn't going to lie, so I told her that yes, he was my husband. She was a bit sheepish, but I assured her our plan would be put into action and her issues resolved. We did accomplish our goal, but this incident does point out some of the challenges of spouses working together in a business.

I mentioned earlier that as I started my new business I essentially knew I didn't want to work with my spouse every day. That is no slight to him or our relationship. It is a realization I have come to after 27-plus years of marriage and with the experience of already having worked together. Additionally, we have very different skill sets and very different ways of looking at situations, which might lead to conflict as business owners. While it was something we enjoyed when we were younger, we were also part of a larger team. We weren't working together side by side every day. We also weren't trying to build our future off the same financial platform. In fact, that had been one of our concerns. Both of us losing our jobs if the company had issues would put us at risk.

I ended up leaving first, even though I really didn't have a desire to leave. An opportunity came my way, however, and I didn't want to pass it by and always wonder if I should have taken it. In hindsight, it was a wonderful decision. Not because that job was so great—it wasn't—but because it gave me the background, contacts and mindset that allowed me to take the director of marketing role that gave me much of the experience for what I do today in business coaching.

If you are a mid-career individual looking to maybe start a business and you want to work with your spouse that is fantastic. I congratulate you. Let's look at a few examples of typical mid-career opportunities and the joys, challenges and opportunities that come with the experience.

Typical Second Careers

One type of second career is opening a bed and breakfast. They became very popular, especially in the 1980s, and many sprang up around the U.S. and around the world.

The challenges with a bed and breakfast type of business include:

+ 24/7 job—With many bed and breakfasts, you live at the same place where you work. This means you not only live together but also work together 24/7. This can put huge strains on a marriage. Think of permanent retirement, yet you are both still working and trying to make money. You often have no space to call your own. Yes, you can escape to your bedroom, but that space can become confining and claustrophobic. This can happen in many different industries, but it is often seen in businesses like hobby shops, campgrounds, bed and breakfasts and seasonal business ventures.

+ Financial investment—When many bed and breakfasts first started, they were in homes where people lived and so the costs to start them were not significant. The owners started small, with one room and then two, etc. Now that first generation of B&B owners wants to retire, and the next owners have all the regular business expenses as well as the debt of buying the investment. That debt can often be the difference between success and failure. I have seen B&Bs make money, but they are often the ones without debt. I have also seen B&Bs with a crushing debt load and owners who are barely making ends meet. This has especially been true in the recent recession, as people minimize travel and those rooms remain vacant; that is money lost each night that can't be recovered.

+ Death of one spouse—What is a lot of work for a couple is a great deal of work for one person. As you plan your business, you need to decide what will happen if one of you can't work, dies or gets sick. You must have a contingency plan, and that contingency plan cannot be to sell the business. Selling the business could take years.

+ Exit strategy—You must have an exit strategy that doesn't involve selling the business quickly. There are no guarantees you will be able to sell unless you are willing to accept pennies on the dollar.

There are also a number of joys and opportunities in owning a bed and breakfast:

• Working with your spouse—The ability to work with your spouse can be exciting. You are working with someone you trust, the commute to work is nonexistent and you get to meet wonderful people. You also have the opportunity to talk with people from various cultures and share your love of your town and community with those who are new to the area.

• Fulfillment—The ability to build something together is truly fulfilling. Building your future, doing something new and being able to work alongside your spouse is fun. You grow together, you serve together and those you serve get the opportunity to watch what you do. For many people, watching you work together might be the first time they have ever seen what a joy it can be to work with your spouse. That leaves a legacy that goes beyond just providing a place to stay.

• Flexibility—You have the ability to build your business so someone else can provide services to your guests, meaning that you won't have to spend all your time living and working together. That concept is critical to your mental and physical well-being. If hiring is done correctly, you then have the opportunity to travel, get to see the world and enjoy the benefits of having a business that can run without you.

Another type of second-career business is real estate. The owner buys a house, fixes it up, rents it out and pays on a mortgage for 15 to 30 years. When it is paid off, they have leveraged their time and money into money for retirement (which is when the mortgages are usually paid off). This has made a great number of people wealthy. They are often risk takers who are willing to leverage their time and skills into maintaining the house and keeping it in shape for their renters.

Reasons for Launching a Second Career

The second-career family business is an awesome way to invest that part of your life. Often the children are older and have left home or are at the stage where they are less dependent. My parents did the second-career business. My dad had been a salesperson for General Electric for 19 years, and both he and they came to the conclusion that he had no more career advancement opportunities within GE. He could stay in the same role for the years to come, but that wasn't appealing to my father. He was never the type to sit around and leave things status quo.

He found a mobile home park that was for sale in the hills of California. He emptied my parents' short-term savings account of $1,000 (this was in the early 1970s when $1,000 was a lot of money) and left his paid job. He and Mom went on to make a thriving business out of the venture. For the first year, they traveled up to the park each day (it was about an hour away from our house), worked and came home in the evening. As I look back, I realize the level of risk they took, not just in being able to pay the bills, but for their future as well. IRAs and 401(k)s had not been created. Savings and leveraging yourself was the primary way of securing retirement, especially since Dad had left the safety net of the big company. Dad knew they would never be able to retire comfortably without taking some risk.

One of my favorite stories to tell happened about a year later when I was a senior in high school. While most kids move out of their parents' home at the end of high school, my parents moved out on me. They gave me the option of moving an hour away and living with them or finding a place to live for the last semester of high school. That was an easy decision for me: I found some friends to live with for that eight-month period until graduation and then the summer. I then left for college and essentially, due to many circumstances, never returned to live at home.

After moving into the mobile home park, my parents worked their business essentially day and night. The office was in their home and they did all the work that needed to be done. This was a high-end mobile home park, carved into the hillside of Foresthill, California. The scenery was beautiful, the homes were nice and my parents made a living. Dad was handy so he was able to do much of the work from cleaning the septic systems to building new areas for mobile homes to move into. The park became profitable.

As a side note, they did have partners in this venture. The partners were old friends who actually lived across the street from us. That part of the venture did not work out as well as it could have. The partners were also in a second-career/husband and wife situation. Their work ethic, skills and business acumen were not at the same level with the same focus as my parents'. If you think family-owned business environments can be difficult, partnerships can be even harder.

Forming a partnership is sort of like getting married. After the partnership agreement is signed (hopefully you have one; if you don't, have one drawn up *before* tensions arise), the reality of living and working together will create strain. Unlike in a marriage where you hopefully love each other, in a partnership there is a like—but not that love to help you get past the rough spots. Many partnerships don't work for the same reasons that family-owned businesses can be a challenge: lack of operating agreements, having no one specific person in charge, having no financial plan and more.

I am often asked whether a partnership in a business should be 50/50. That is a hard question. If you do go 50/50, then who or what breaks the tie when you disagree about a decision? Essentially someone must be the president/CEO who makes the decisions for the business, and the other partner must trust the president/CEO to make things happen; otherwise you get stuck in a spot where nothing moves forward. Those partnerships that work with a 50/50 split are ones that have worked out the "what if's" in advance: Who breaks the tie? What are the roles and responsibilities? What happens if we do disagree? What is the process for mediation?

My parents moved on from their mobile home park second-career family business to a construction business that did construction around mobile homes. They were able to sell the mobile home business at a profit, which is often a challenge for the second-career business owner. They were fortunate to find an opportunity and take advantage of it. As they essentially moved into their third career, Dad created an even more optimal environment: He could work when he wanted and take off time when he wanted. The reality is that they worked probably 10 months per year, so they were able to travel in their motor home for a couple of months every year.

The construction business had its own challenges. One of them was that many of my parents' clients were older and lonely. My mom's job for certain clients was to essentially keep them company and out of Dad's hair while he worked. This became especially true for certain clients who if Mom wasn't around would answer the door totally nude looking for additional "help" around the house. Dad wasn't really interested in those types of benefits of owning his own business! It really goes to show the unusual situations that come from being a business owner—family business or not.

Facing Challenges

Here are some of the challenges for the second-career family business:

+ Most of the time all your eggs are now in this second-career business. Your future, your retirement and your livelihood are all wrapped up in this business. That creates a level of emotion that can affect interaction with your spouse, partners and others around you. Failure can be catastrophic financially and sometimes for the marriage.
  › I have stated this before, but it bears repeating: Run your business as a business, not as a family venture. Separate work from home as best you can. Have a plan for business growth and work the plan. Know your roles and know your strengths.

Play to those roles and strengths. If one is good at sales, make
sure they sell. If one is good at behind-the-scenes details, then
allow them to work the details. Create rules of the game for
how you work together. Get
someone outside the business
to provide the clarity needed for
both your personal life and your
business. Countless times when
I have worked with married
couples, I will recommend a

> *Run your business
> as a business,
> not as a family venture.
> Separate work from
> home as best you can.*

course of action that is exactly the same as what the spouse
has recommended previously. But when I mention it, it will
be put into action, unlike when the spouse has recommended
the same course of action. In other words, they will listen
to an outsider, not the spouse. If your spouse is like that, let
an outside advisor help you navigate the difficult waters of a
family business.

› Determine the non-negotiables in the business. This means
what you will not compromise on. On the surface this may
sound obvious, yet when you are in the heat of a situation,
it is not so obvious. Non-negotiables can be different for
each family, but can range from values and integrity to family
vacations. There is no rule book here; these are the things you
care most about. Be realistic and flexible when you discuss your
non-negotiables. For example, if family dinner time is a non-
negotiable, realize it may not work every day of the week. (If
you think business interferes with dinner time, try high school
activities.) Your compromise might be that Wednesday dinner
is always a family dinner. Another example might be exercise. If
daily exercise is a non-negotiable, I suggest a morning workout;
it's too easy for the afternoon workout to get compromised.

✦ Too much togetherness. It is often joked that when one person
retires (often the husband) the other spouse goes and finds a job

to get out of the house and away from the retiree. This situation is very true in a family business. You are around each other constantly. At first, one of you may be delivering the product. For example, if the husband is an electrician, he might be in the field working with customers. He can't remain in the field on a permanent basis, however. He will need to step out of being an electrician and into being the business owner, which involves looking at the bigger picture and not the outlet needing to be installed. If you are in business with your child, the idiosyncrasies and differences that drove you crazy during the teenage years might still drive you crazy, which can be a problem if you'll be around him or her more often.

COACH'S CORNER
Ask Questions

The one piece of advice I would offer is this: Take off the blinders when you're researching any business you want to buy. Talk to others who have worked in the same type of business. Don't be afraid to ask the hard questions like:

- What is the work week like?
- What is it like working with your spouse?
- Would you do it again?
- What are the financials?
- What is the profit?
- How easy is it to sell?

The second-career family business is occasionally begun by a couple in their post-children years. They understand the workings of a good relationship and how each other operates, and have navigated through the issues of understanding the strengths and weaknesses of their partner. One business that exemplifies this is a husband/wife team that had worked in the wealth management and health care industry for many years. They had gone through all the stages of understanding business and what it was all about and had the energy and perseverance to start—after the age of 60—what was essentially a third career for the husband. They saw the power of leveraging their time for passive income (income that will pay you long after you have stopped working full time). They also had the financial security to try something new, and even though it had some downside, there was less than for other businesses.

It was truly fun to watch them grow. They did it right. They made sure they had advisors around them to navigate the waters of a new business. As their coach, it was fun for me to watch them learn the new aspects of business. Remember—it is one thing to be an employee and quite another to be the employer! They learned how to test and measure, create goals, achieve those goals and wow their clients. Every year they come to the annual planning workshop to plan their next year. Every year I see growth in them, their business and their ability to balance what they want to do with how much they want to play. Right now they are planning for 12 weeks of vacation a year, essentially one week per month. They are the success story.

Now it doesn't mean things weren't hard, there were no struggles, and the "oops factor" didn't raise its head. It also doesn't mean that the strength of their marriage wasn't tested. There were and are still times (as in all quality relationships) that frustration builds, communication falters and tension rises. Situations at home spill over to work; situations at work spill over to home. The success is in open and trusting communication, knowing they are in this together, and the staying power of walking the journey together.

How do you handle the "OOPS" factor:

1. Do not overreact: Overreacting to a situation creates knee jerk decision that most peple regret. Take a deep breath, talk to that

The "Oops Factor"

The oops factor is those "I didn't see this coming, didn't plan for this issue and now have a problem" situations. Examples would include having a month-to-month lease and the landlord wants you to move by the end of the month; failing to back up your computer regularly to prevent disaster when your hard drive crashes; and having your key employee walk out the door or not show up for work with no notice.

outside business advisor. Sleep on it—i.e., let some time pass. Depending on the situation that might be an hour, a day or longer. Time has a way of providing perspectives. Oops can be magnified by decisions made in the heat of the moment.

2. Lay out a written plan: The plan might be for the next 2 days, yet the simple process of writing down the plan, and then talking it over with someone will calm the thought processes and help you think through options. The plan will then allow you to act on a more rational course of action.

3. Step back: If you were counseling someone else on this issue— without the emotion you now have, what you you counsel them? Stepping back gives you perspective and allows the better decision making process. What questions do you ask yourself when an "oops" happens?

4. Scale it: How big of an oops is this? When they happen we tend to think this situation is "huge". On a scale of one to ten—it is an eleven. Yet when you have stepped back, haven't over reacted, laid out a plan—you now have perspective. I have a friend who owns a business and they had not renewed the lease on their building. They were notified they had to be out of the building within 2 weeks. This wasn't an easy feat, they had equipment to

move, a business to run, a busy time of year and all the ramifications of a move. Now moving quickly wasn't what they planned to accomplish over Christmas, yet the end result was the opportunity to purchase another building (a dream he had always had) get more space for the office and room to store equipment and a better operating environment. If he had over reacted, not laid out a plan and looked at the big picture his decision process might not have allowed him the opportunity to achieve a dream. For this one on the scale of one to ten, it turned out to be a 2. It created a few long days and nights, but the end result is a wonderful result.

Having an Exit Strategy

It was good that my parents had the vision (although it was blurry at times) to create their own business. That leverage is what has allowed my mom to live comfortably in her retirement years. While that business ownership is in part what protected them, it is also what killed my father. He was diagnosed with mesothelioma, which is asbestos-related cancer. He was exposed on the farm as a kid and also through his work with the pipes at the mobile home park. One never knows how business or life will go so it's important to have a plan. That plan needs to take into account the potential of one of you not living out your golden years. Without that plan, all of your time, energy and work may not help you achieve your dreams.

The ability to exit the second-career business is critical. It often depends on the time frame you want to exit. Starting that second career at age 55 and wanting to work another 10 years will require you to really look at your ability to leverage your skills and the business, as well as the future market for the business. The baby boomer generation creates both an advantage and a disadvantage to the second-career business. The advantage is the possibility of many boomers being ready to do something other than what they have done for the first years of their career. They have capital with which they can invest. They often know business as they have worked for someone else for 20 or 30 years, and they are ready to make that change.

The downside is the same: Many boomers are getting ready to retire, they have had businesses and there are many businesses on the market. What will be required of your business to sell it in these economic times? What really needs to happen is you must stand out from the others, be different, show profitability and demonstrate that efficient systems are in place. Make sure your business is truly marketable, which again requires the owner to make sure the blinders are off and they are not looking at the business through rose-colored glasses.

CHAPTER 11

Turning a Hobby into a Business

Some family-owned businesses are built on a hobby. The owner's love for doing something led to the creation of a business.

A good example of this type of business is Mrs. Fields Cookies. Debbi Fields loved to cook and create wonderful cookies. Everyone suggested that she take her hobby of baking and start a business. She was able to turn her hobby, love and passion for baking into a new love and passion—that of running a business. She is probably the exception rather than the rule in hobby businesses, however.

Now that doesn't mean money can't be made, bills paid and a livelihood created, but the profits generated probably would not be considered wealth. One of the real challenges for the hobby business owner is to determine what they really want out of this business. It's not that the concept is different for other business owners, but the hobby business owner can often end up hating the hobby if he or she doesn't make the right transition. There are many examples of hobbies that became businesses; there are few examples of hobbies that became successful businesses in the sense of making money and lasting more than five to seven years.

Other examples are auto body work, car racing, craft work, cooking and working with animals. One of the biggest challenges with the hobby turned business is becoming profitable. Mrs. Fields became profitable, but probably close to 90 percent of hobby businesses don't. I am not talking about the hobby business owner who makes $20,000 and uses it to pay some bills. The profit I am referring to is building a level of wealth, putting money away for education or retirement and paying themselves more than what amounts to minimum wage.

Some of the primary reasons hobby business owners don't become profitable is the owner can't give up the craft aspect of the hobby and often people won't pay the true value of what that hobby is worth. Carving a table out of wood takes hundreds of hours, yet the average individual is not willing to pay thousands of dollars so the craftsman receives the wage needed to be able to live, pay the bills and grow the business. In addition, while the craftsman is spending time creating the masterpiece of a wooden table, they are not marketing that product because they don't have the time or even the skill set to engage in marketing.

This leads to discounting, which leads to a decrease in revenue. It is very hard to become profitable with a hobby business and receive the true return on investment that makes it a profitable business and allows you to achieve the goals and objectives you have identified for that business. If your goal is to make a little spending money from your hobby, that's awesome. If your goal is to make a living, step back and look at the hobby as a business, and then make it a business.

The owners of one business I worked with both had full-time professional jobs and careers. Yet they had a passion for a retail boutique type of business. They knew and understood the retail side of the business and did a great job at setting up the store, getting merchandise, and building a wonderful culture and a wonderful clientele, yet they could not maintain a level of profitability in the store. When we analyzed the profit and loss statement, it became evident that due to the debt load they carried and the need for them to hire out all the staff, it essentially had no hope of being profitable under the current structure. The sad part of this story is they really loved the store, but due to family obligations and their full-time professions, they were required to sell their business. They lost quite a bit of money in the transaction.

The moral to this story is to really look at the pro forma financial statements prior to starting a business, especially a hobby business. Know what your debt load will cost you in cash and understand the impact of your involvement or, in this case, lack of day-to-day involvement. The owners did so much right, yet in the long run their business didn't work. Fortunately they are quick learners, and I expect they will start another venture soon and will apply much of what they have learned.

Selling hobby businesses becomes almost impossible if the owner/craftsman has not hired someone who can reproduce the business product without the business owner. No one wants to buy a business that is profitable, yet solely reliant on the skill or craft of the business owner. That type of arrangement has less than a 5 percent chance of succeeding. Especially in a hobby type of business, you need to determine the exit strategy for the business before you spend time, energy and years building something that will leave you frustrated and broke at the end. Now with that said, it can be done. You can build a profitable hobby business that supports you, your family, your investments and your future. You must be deliberate and you must be the business owner first and the hobbyist second.

Having a family business can be very fulfilling. If you and your spouse/children/family get along, love working together and have a dream, this can be the fulfillment of that dream. Never let anyone squash that dream. Dreams that become fulfilled are done so when the dreamer is wide awake, has a plan, executes that plan and understands that some dreams can turn into nightmares if not executed correctly.

COACH'S CORNER

Inc. magazine's "7 Rules for Avoiding Conflicts of Interest in a Family Business"

Rule 1: Don't put family members on the payroll if they're not working in the company or truly contributing to the company.

Rule 2: Don't create two classes of employees—family vs. non-family.

Rule 3: Be careful not to abuse family relationships.

Rule 4: Communicate honestly and openly with employees, i.e., no secrets.

Rule 5: Don't confuse family and business decisions.

Rule 6: Establish healthy boundaries between family and business.

Rules 7: Use family councils to address family matters.

PART THREE

Relationships in a Family Business

Many of the biggest challenges with running a family business arise because of the relationships within families. With another job, you can leave work at the office and not have to worry as much about bringing the job home, but when your co-workers live under the same roof or are related to you, work and family issues can become intertwined. Your childhood relationships with siblings, parental interactions, self-image and generational thought processes all affect relationships in a family business.

The chapters in this part point out some of these challenges and provide pointers for navigating some of those difficult situations.

CHAPTER 12

How do I Fire My Wife (or Husband)?

That is a question I am often asked by husbands, wives, parents and siblings. They love each other, but working together isn't working. Sarah and Tom had been married about 12 years and they had two children who were under age 6 at the time. Tom was the technician in the business and he was very good at what he did. What wasn't happening was billing, answering the phone, ordering parts and keeping the office (which happened to be in their home) running. Sarah had lost her job, so they figured what better way to help the business than for her to take all those office tasks off of Tom's shoulders.

It was a good thought, but it didn't work out in real life. Sarah, although very outgoing, strongly disliked Tom's business. She wasn't motivated to do anything other than what was required, and as a result tension built between them. After three years of Sarah working in the business (and hating it more every day), they decided they needed to get her out of the business. The balancing act of having the business at home, technicians in the house and young children was becoming a recipe for disaster and divorce. Sarah had to answer the phone while driving the kids to school and at one point was so distracted that she almost drove off the road with the kids in the back seat. That became one of the many warning signals that change was required.

It took time, openness, coaching and strong goal setting to finally make the change. They hired Denise to take over all those responsibilities that had been given to Sarah. Denise worked out of their home, which still wasn't perfect, but it did allow Sarah to separate herself from the day-to-day reality of the business, focus on finding herself a job and turn the family environment back into a pleasant place to be.

What did it take to make that happen?

+ Honesty regarding what each person enjoys doing and their actual contribution to the business.
+ Occasionally a third party to ask the hard questions and help work through the issues.
+ A strong vision for the business and how each person fits or doesn't fit.
+ Determination of what is more important—the business or the marriage. This may sound like a trick question, but not everyone will agree as to what should be first.
+ Detailed roles and responsibilities and complete annual reviews of how each of you is doing in the business. Provide input and recommendations, just like you would for any other employee. In other words, the more this is structured like an employee relationship, the more success you will have and the easier it is for each party to see that it is or isn't working.
+ A transition plan both for the job the spouse is doing and for what they will do after the transition. This can be a big hit to the ego, so coming up with something else the spouse can do to be productive is critical.

• Patience. This change may not happen overnight. In the above story it took about 10 months to make the transition. Each party must want the transition to take place and be willing to have the honest conversation required to make it happen.

Separating Work and Home

How do you actually separate work from your personal life? That really depends on each family business. With one couple I coached, the husband essentially refused to talk about work when they got home. His wife often wanted to reflect on the day, review activities for the next day and make plans, but the husband refused. They essentially needed to create rules of the game for how to operate and when to have debriefing and planning sessions. He was done when he walked out the door, but she needed that discussion.

Set aside time either each day or each week for planning and review. After all, if you didn't live together, you would have to set up a time for this discussion. The sooner you make it happen, the easier life will become. Now that sounds easy to do, yet in practice can be very difficult. It really depends on the individual personalities and the relationships between each of them. Sometimes bringing things home works; it is a time to unwind over a glass of wine, determine how the day has gone and plan for the coming days and weeks. However, that seldom works if there are children at home wanting attention from the parents.

If there are children of any age at home, leave work at the office. Yes, there is value to having general discussions about the workday over the dinner table with the children. That provides teaching time to kids, which is invaluable, especially if you see them potentially being involved in the business in the future. Yet that should not be the time to debate policies, talk about personnel or deal with critical business issues that have the potential of being heated.

Another family business did just the opposite of the couple mentioned at the beginning of the chapter. They had small children at home and the lines were far more blurred regarding home vs. business. Although they had a nanny for most day care, there were times that the needs of the kids during the day required personal time; therefore, work was accomplished during the evening when the kids were asleep or otherwise engaged. This husband/wife duo allocated time every evening to touch base and to make sure they had communicated any issues that arose during the day. They worked to table controversial discussions, which was successful much of the time. This practice did help make their mornings a bit more informed and less stressful.

Spouse-Only Time

For couples who work together, is your conversation only about the kids? Only about work? For the family business owner it is even more imperative to maintain things in common other than business (and the children if applicable). Make sure the business is not your whole life. At least once a month, go out as a couple, have fun and do something new—*don't* talk about business. Pursue a hobby or interest and get out of your comfort zone. Make sure this time is scheduled. Time away that isn't scheduled seldom happens. Weeks, months and years pass, and time can never be recovered.

My husband does not like to dance. He says he has two left feet. However, one Valentine's Day a group of our friends were taking a swing dance class together. Being the good guy that he is—and as my Valentine's gift, which then became a set of four lessons with the same group—he came to the classes with me. Did he ever really learn to love to dance? Not yet! However, he was willing to get out of his comfort zone, do something new, have fun with friends and be willing to stumble around on those two left feet.

COACH'S CORNER

Making It Work

+ Create a system that works for your family. There isn't a right or wrong answer, but there is an answer that works for you.
+ Review how your system is working on a regular basis. Quarterly is recommended, but it should be done at least annually.
+ Be willing to change the system as business and life changes.
+ Avoid having anyone report directly to a member of his or her family. If you do, have specific ways of handling conflict, non-performance and accountability.
+ Don't assume good familial relationships automatically translate to good business relationships.
+ Make sure family members are qualified.
+ Don't be afraid to bring in outside help and perspectives. Outside professionals can be useful to establish day-to-day policy and long-term succession plans, and to resolve conflict.
+ Have a weekly meeting with the family and have at least a monthly business meeting. This is the key to communication. Set up a time, day and agenda for the meeting. It is critical. *A Wall Street Journal* article by Bruce Feiler discussed "taking solutions from the workplace and transferring them to the home" through accountability checklists, family branding sessions, efficient conflict resolution sessions and more. These concepts work well at the office and can have a place at home.
+ Don't make assumptions about any family member. Assuming gets you in trouble.
+ Other areas for regular review:
  + Roles and responsibilities
  + Rules of the game for how the family operates
  + Wills and estate plans
  + Desires and goals for each family member. Each person will have a sense of feeling trapped at some point. A non-family employee can decide to get another job any day. The family member doesn't always have that luxury or feel they have that luxury. Be available to discuss the topic on a regular basis (maybe annually). If nothing else, it will provide a vehicle for discussion that may lead to an exit strategy if needed.

Get out and do something! Those outside interests are good for you, your relationship and your business. People don't want to do business with boring people who are focused on just one thing. They want to do business with well-rounded people with outside interests. Colleges don't just look for academic ability; they look for community involvement, outside hobbies and interests, and so do your customers. They might buy from you once, but the connection comes when they see the other things you do, your other interests and what motivates you outside the business environment. Doing something new and different also keeps your spouse engaged as you have something to talk about, something to do and something to give back to the family outside of the day-to-day business.

Bringing Kids to Work

This issue creates strife in many families and businesses. Some people don't believe kids should be in a place of business, and others say it is their business and therefore they can do what they want.

Here are some questions to ask yourself:

- Customers are first. (Remember, they pay the bills.) Do they care?
- What image does seeing kids at work give your customers?
- How well-behaved are the kids, i.e., what impact are they having on the business, customers and other employees? "Well-behaved" is often in the eyes of the beholder; what one considers well-behaved someone else might not. The true beholders are your customers and employees. The reality, however, is that what is cute at age 3 is annoying at age 9, yet parents allow the behavior at both ages. If customers and employees don't believe the children are well-behaved, you have a decision to make—change the behavior of your children or understand the consequences, which can be losing customers, losing employees or both.

- How are the kids impacting your productivity? That is, are you taking a six-hour day and making it a 10-hour day due to attending to kids? What about your employees' productivity?
- Are you creating a good environment for the kids? Or are they not allowed to be kids (always in the corner and not allowed to talk, have fun or run around)?

I have spoken to many children and grandchildren whose families owned businesses. Some love the family business; some detest the business and what it has meant to them. In one family I interviewed, the grandchildren were very proud of the business, what it meant to the family and the opportunity it presented as they grew up. Many of them looked forward to the potential of being able to work in it after they graduated from college and had some experience in other industries. It has also provided guidance in the sense that many people in the community knew the family so the kids and then the grandkids knew if they did something out of line that someone in the family would hear about it.

Yet that same environment is what makes some subsequent generations rebel from any involvement in the family business. It always overshadowed everything they did and could do, which became confining and stifling. This rebellion can last for years, decades or their entire lives.

Some of the above questions about children in the workplace could be asked about the family dog (or cat, bird, monkey, etc.) that goes to work as well. One business owner brought two of his labrador retrievers to work all the time. The office manager was being saddled with walking the animals, the employees were tired of them being around and some customers were actually hesitant to come into the office when the dogs were present. Although the owner didn't like the reality, he needed to make a decision about what was more important. Again, there isn't a right or wrong answer, but whatever the answer is, you must accept it and move on.

If the dogs are more important, then make sure the dogs are away when some customers visit or know that your revenue may be impacted by their presence. It is only when you complain about loss of revenue, lack of new customers and employee turnover due to the animals and won't make a change that the line has been crossed. You are no longer a responsible business owner but a whiney business owner who isn't willing to take responsibility for the situation he finds himself in.

COACH'S CORNER

Parents and Children

Parents, you can't dictate what your children will do with their lives. (OK, you can, but it probably isn't the wisest step.) Stop trying, stop giving guilt trips and stop holding on to what you want your kids to do. If it is right for them, they will come back to the business. If it isn't, they will go on to other productive things in their lives. Whatever their decision, let it be their decision. I cry inwardly every time I see a family business where the parents (or even the second or third generation) want to see their kids take over the business and the kids have no interest. The wall this creates affects the relationship in all ways and seldom leads to a positive conclusion. By allowing the kids to leave and pursue another career and life, they will sometimes return to the family business, older, wiser and ready to take on the challenge. This is a far better result for you, them and the business than guilting them into staying around.

Time Management and the Family Business

Time management is a challenge for many people, whether or not they are business owners. There are countless books on ways to best manage your time. Stephen Covey's *The Seven Habits of Highly Effective People* and *First Things First* and David Allen's *Getting Things Done* are great at helping you look at the tasks you do and making a determination for where you actually want to spend your time.

Sally was in a high-pressure business. She had people, email, phones and work all demanding her attention on a regular basis. Her interrupt factor was extremely high, but because she worked in the contract department of her company, her ability to focus on the details was critical. We first met in a group setting where the topic was time management and how to get more accomplished in the time available without working an 18-hour day. (That wasn't my title, but that is what she was looking for.)

We discussed the concept of being able to close the door of her office, turn off email and the phones and focus on doing one thing without interruption for an hour. She erupted. "That isn't possible with my job. People stand at my door waiting for answers, and the phone is constantly ringing. That won't work!" I paused, allowed her to finish and asked her a question: "So what is happening right now while you are in this workshop?" (which happened to be five hours long). Sally was silent for a moment and then stated, "Well, things are piling up while I am in here." My challenge to her was to just try it—if it didn't work, she could go back to how she was handling things now. I chose not to challenge her further in front of her peers at that time and we moved on to another topic.

The following week during a conversation Sally started off with an apology for coming on so strong during the workshop. It turned out that she had tried my suggestion. The previous day she had communicated to her team that she had some projects to complete. She was going to close her door, put a "Do Not Disturb" sign on it, close email and also set her phone to do not disturb. In that hour she accomplished more than she had in the previous three days combined and was sold on the value of focused time away from interruptions.

In an interview that appeared in *Success* magazine (which I highly recommend you subscribe to), writer and speaker Mike Vardy discussed productivity. He has done a number of studies that indicate the average executive/business owner focuses on one thing for no more than 11 minutes. For every interruption, it takes about 25 minutes to recover where they were and start making progress again.

The concept of multitasking is killing our productivity. It has been proved that our mind cannot multitask. It actually switches gears from one topic to another but doesn't truly multitask. We have all been in situations where we have been concentrating to get something accomplished, been interrupted and then either had to start over in our thought process or wondered where we were and never got back to that same state. Mike Vardy also stated in his research that multitasking actually diminishes our IQ by 10 points.

Yes, there are situations that require us to juggle a number of things at one time. I used to be called the "queen of multitasking." I could be processing multiple things at one time fairly well and keep all the balls up in the air. However, when I needed to focus, complete a project, plan for a conference or review a sales proposal, that was all I did. The door was closed, email ignored and phones put on do not disturb because I knew that missing one small item could be the difference between success and failure. I also had the benefit of being able to work from home a couple days per week and I scheduled my focus times for those days.

Who is running your day—you or others?

Time management is essentially about self-management. Who is running your day—you or others? Do you determine your action items for the day the day before? If not, then consider planning tomorrow today, next week this week, next month this month. Make sure you leave time to plan. Without planning you put yourself and your life in a reactive rather than proactive mode. You wonder why things happen to you, why you need to work late, why it is taking longer than you anticipated. Most of these situations are due to lack of planning.

Have you decided that you can manage time? Asking this question gets mixed reactions of yes and no. The reality is no, you can't manage time. Time moves on no matter what we do. What we can do is manage ourselves. Self-management is the most critical aspect. As an initial step, figure out what you are avoiding, then do it first and get it done. Plan your day. If you say it doesn't work, then step back and take a hard look as to why. Let's say you are in a situation with a high interrupt factor; then plan for it. Get in early and get those projects done before everyone else arrives. Put on your calendar time to complete your action list for the day. If you haven't planned for when the action items will get accomplished, you have a much lower chance of getting things done.

At least once a month schedule a family business meeting (this is over and above your personal family meeting). Yes, even if it is your siblings, children etc. with whom you are in business. Plan out the activities, events and engagements for the month. Have a calendar that everyone has access to and lay out events for the month (or quarter). This simple process will save you time, agony and misunderstandings. Incorporate both business and personal. If the business is open to customers outside the normal 9 to 5, this becomes even more critical. For example, Mom's birthday dinner gets planned for 6 p.m. on Tuesday and that is John's day to close up the shop, which doesn't close until 8 p.m. Planning ahead and taking everyone's schedule into consideration helps to avoid the situation where Mom is upset that John arrived late, John is upset that this is the fourth dinner that has been planned on his night to work late and John's wife wonders once again why they get the short stick.

One of my clients had been planning to attend a two-day workshop that extended over a Friday and Saturday. It was held only once a year and he had the dates on his calendar for probably six months. As the time grew closer, confirmations of attendance were sent out and he went home about three weeks prior to the event excited about his opportunity to attend. The big pin that came out to burst his bubble really made an impact. That weekend was when he had kid duty all weekend for all but one of his kids. His wife and daughter were planning a weekend away and he was in charge. Oops.

In case you are wondering, he didn't attend the workshop, but he did put the dates for next year's workshop on the family calendar, which they now utilize. Every month they sit down and plan out four to six weeks of events, no matter how big or small. This planning session has become a family affair and has minimized one aspect of stress in their lives. It is also teaching the kids about planning, scheduling and compromising since not everyone gets to do what they want when they want. That is a lesson everyone needs to learn.

Another lesson on time management for the family business is about using dual or triple resources on a single activity. Having two or three people doing the same activity within the business is a tremendous waste of time and resources. Every business ends up with this time sink. Examples include:

- Two people go to a networking event and rather than dividing up and working the room separately, they talk to everyone together.
- Meetings of all kinds. Yes, there is a time and a place for both of you to attend, but that should be the exception rather than the rule. If you have a strong set of roles and responsibilities, such as one is the engineer, the other is the head of customer service and the prospect wants to meet both, then go for it. However, what I see more often than not is the head of customer service goes to the engineering meeting just because it's always been done that way (even though it began because there wasn't a team in each area). Stop trying to do the other person's job. Each person (family member or not) needs to be held accountable for doing their job, period.
- Vendor/supplier negotiations. Again, unless there is a designated role for each family member or person present, don't have people tag along just because. They need a specific role and responsibility in the meeting. If you do double up, make sure there is a clear purpose, such as playing good cop/bad cop.

Roles and Self-Esteem

In the book *First, Break All the Rules: What the World's Greatest Managers Do Differently,* authors Marcus Buckingham and Curt Coffman talk about what makes great managers. One section specifically addresses the need for well-rounded leaders: "As they struggle to carve out their success, the last thing on their mind was to become well rounded. They may have been aware of their own shortcomings, but none of them worked at turning these shortcomings into strengths. They knew what a hopeless waste of time that would be. So they did something else instead: they looked for a partner." The authors provided examples of Walt Disney and his brother Roy; David Packard and William Hewlett; and Bill Gates and Paul Allen, saying, "Each partnership was effective precisely because where one partner was blunt, the other was sharp. The partnerships were well rounded, not the individuals."

This often perfectly identifies the partnership that can happen in a business with spouses. What initially attracted them to each other were often not the similarities but the differences. The old saying "opposites attract" is true in many marriages I have seen. This is even truer in family businesses with the husband and wife as the owners. One is frugal and conservative; the other doesn't worry about money and has the vision. One is sociable and loves to sell; the other would rather not be around people they don't know.

> *Each partnership was effective precisely because where one partner was blunt, the other was sharp. The partnerships were well rounded, not the individuals.*

The challenge becomes in allowing the partnership to blossom on the strengths of what the two become and not continually micromanage the other individual. What often happens is both parties end up trying to do the same job; rather than leveraging their time and skills, they have slowed down the business by duplicating tasks.

This happens constantly. At networking events, Jim loves to engage with others, seek out new business and understand what is going on in the market. Janice tags along because she knows the business needs sales but she doesn't enjoy these events. She finds them loud, doesn't like to meet people she doesn't know and lacks confidence in how to articulate the business. The end result is both lose. Jim knows Janice doesn't like these events. He tries to make her feel comfortable, but that takes away from his networking since his complete focus isn't on the event. Janice loses credibility because she doesn't say much and lacks engagement in the conversation. They leave the event and discuss on the way home how networking is a waste of time. This type of scenario plays out often in the family business.

There are multiple examples of this type of behavior—meetings with vendors, meetings with customers, internal operational meetings with the team. It doesn't mean there isn't a time and place for both parties; it just means you aren't joined at the hip for all business activities. There are times when showing the family unit is absolutely critical to the branding of the business or closing a deal. Regular discussions need to take place on who should go, why and what the purpose is for multiple family members to attend.

Jim and Janice could try an alternative approach if it is imperative that both attend. Determine for both of you the 10-second, 60-second and 3-minute version of what to say at a networking event. There are fantastic books available for this training. One resource I highly recommend is Jeffrey Gitomer's Little Book series, which addresses selling, networking, trust and other subjects. He has a practical, light, direct and pragmatic approach to these topics and will help you learn how to make the most of all the interactions you have with people.

Even if both of you are good at an activity, it isn't necessary for both of you to be involved. A good way to look at these activities starts with understanding the value each person brings to the table. Determining roles and having both a financial budget and a time budget, or calendar, is critical.

Let's look at the value of time. What would you rather lose—time or money? Think it through; your answer will reveal where your business's growth stands. A majority of people would rather lose time. In *The Seven Habits of Highly Effective People*, Stephen Covey talks about time and how we spend it, or as I say, lose it.

The answer to the question is we should rather lose money. We can always get money back, but time once spent can never be earned back. That concept is startling and contrary for many of you reading this book. The thought of losing money is scary and unthinkable. Some of you might drive 5 miles to save 2 cents per gallon on gas. You actually lose both time and money in that situation because it usually costs you more in gas to make the drive than you save and if you place any value on your time, you have really lost.

My clients all go through the following exercise:

What is an hour of your time worth? Most of them either way overestimate the value or way underestimate the value. Let's say they start by saying $48 per hour. (They get to that number usually by calculating what they want to bring home in pay, which is often the magical number of $100,000, and then divide by 2080, which is 40 hours per week multiplied by 52 weeks in a year.) Now assume one of your big challenges in the business is lack of time. (I haven't yet found a business owner who stated that wasn't one of their primary business challenges.) As the business owner, you likely

What is an hour of your time worth?

know your product best and are great at conducting product sales, so why are you spending so much time doing jobs that pay $15 or $20 per hour? What would having another 10 to 15 hours per week to leverage yourself and your business to the next level and generate another $100,000, $1 million or $5 million in revenue be worth to you?

Kim was the owner of a heating and ventilation business. She continued to believe that she needed to do the books for the business. She needed to know where all the revenue came from, where the money was being spent and what the cash balance was. It was taking up close to 20 hours per week to get everything done. As a result, she had little time for marketing, business planning and business growth, and her family time was becoming stressful because she didn't have energy for her kids. She eventually realized that understanding the revenue, the bills and the cash balance could be done in about one hour a week. She didn't need to enter the transactions to know the totals. She hired a bookkeeper to do the data entry and daily books. She then received reports at the end of each week. She reviewed them, asked questions if something didn't seem right and managed cash flow from a report, not from the anxiety of entering every invoice.

Kim was then able to leverage her time with strategic planning, marketing, team building and hiring. As a result, the business became more profitable than it had been in the last 15 years. She was also able to start leveraging relationships, which grew the company's revenue by over 30 percent. By spending around $15,000 per year, Kim was able to leverage her time to generate around $400,000 in revenue and another $40,000 in profit.

Where do you need to change how you spend your time?

COACH'S CORNER
Time vs. Money

- Determine the value of your time. What is an hour worth? Are you spending it wisely?
- Create a master calendar for your regular activities.
- Sit down and determine how the family is utilizing their time. Is more than one person attending functions, activities and meetings where they aren't necessary?

Marrying into the Business

The business is operational. Employees are in place, the operation runs smoothly but now there is a new team member in town. The new wife or husband is now involved. What will their role be? How does everyone handle this new member of the family and team?

A meeting was scheduled with the owners of a restaurant that had been around for a number of years. Connie and Mike wanted to discuss their team and the challenges with the team. They walked in about 10 minutes late (they had also attended a time management workshop for which they were about 15 minutes late). From the moment they walked into the building, there was tension in the air. They would have been on time, but Connie had to make a stop somewhere else first and then they took the long way to my office.

Shortly after they sat down in my office, the bickering resumed. The business was fine (although I questioned that fact based on the interaction I was observing). They just had team issues and it revolved around Mike and his management style with the various restaurant locations. When issues arose, Connie always wanted to handle the issues, but Mike believed that the managers should be able to handle the situation.

I am not a marriage counselor and counseled them that if they wanted help with their business we could talk; otherwise I could make some recommendations for marriage counselors. They stopped arguing and said their marriage was fine (maybe by their definition). What that statement did accomplish was to get them focused on the business issues instead of their marital issues. According to them, they never bickered when they were outside the business. The conversation continued about how Mike managed the team and how the team members responded when he attempted to either hold them accountable or get things accomplished.

This one-hour drama revealed that they had been married less than two years. Connie had owned the business for many years on her own after the death of her first husband and Mike was new on the scene. Connie had never really communicated to her team that Mike had any level of authority or responsibility over them. She just assumed that because they were married, everyone would know that to be the case. Mike was very qualified, but the team's loyalty was to Sarah, and Mike did things differently from Connie.

They left my office with me shaking my head over how one simple bit of communication would make such a huge difference in the lives of the family and the business. In the short time we talked, they gave countless examples of the misperceptions they had of what each other was doing and why. Getting those topics on the table changed a very adversarial meeting into one where they truly believed they could now work together and resolve their team issues.

These are some of the lessons that can be learned from this example:

- When you bring a new family member into the business, make sure the roles and responsibilities are clearly defined and communicated to everyone, including the family member.
- Communicate, communicate, communicate. Have regular meetings with your spouse, siblings and children with an agenda that addresses the situations of the week, month and quarter. Address the situations before they become problems. Do *not* stick your head in the sand and hope it will go away. *Very, very* seldom do issues go away. They may short term, but like a cut that is not treated properly, there is a good chance it will become infected and the healing process is harder and takes longer. Sometimes limbs need to be severed to save the whole body.
- Listen, listen, listen. Too often listening comes with filters, especially within the family. Long-standing issues that haven't been dealt with create such a filter that neither party can or will listen attentively. Listening means coming to the story with an empty canister of emotion. If you believe you already know what your sister will say, since you have heard it all before, then you have no room in the canister for what she is really saying. What happened in childhood or last weekend outside of work should have nothing to do with the work situation that you are addressing.

Divorce

Divorce is a risk for small companies, particularly when both husband and wife are owners. The business is one more asset to divide (and fight about) in a divorce and may be the primary source of income of one or both spouses. Without an agreement about how an owner can exit the business, a divorce could destroy it. This becomes one of the hard discussions that a family business owner must have when they start the business. Waiting until there is an asset worth fighting about (i.e., when the business is doing well) or until the emotions are running high is not the time to draw up an agreement. Saying it won't happen is shortsighted and foolish. The process of having the discussion actually helps to lay the foundation to ensure it doesn't happen. With an agreement in place, greed plays less of a role and hopefully the business can be salvaged in the process.

Divorce can also challenge the ownership structure of the business if there is no agreement defining how new owners are brought in. Let's say that Bob divorces Karen. As part of the divorce settlement, Karen gets 50 percent of Bob's shares in the business. If Bob and Karen were equal owners previously, now Karen is the majority owner. She has complete control for any decisions requiring a majority vote and can change the dynamic for decisions that require a unanimous vote. This can work for the business if Karen is making decisions based on what is right for the business and not using it to attack Bob. The reality is that you should plan for the potential so you at least have a foundation from which to build (or in this case, tear down). The end result can be keeping the business as a viable, profitable entity that serves the customers and provides value to the owners and the community.

Unmarried co-owners, like siblings or parent/child owners, may also hit a point where they need to break up, which can feel like a divorce depending upon the reasons (money, betrayal, lack of attention, etc.). When there are no agreements in place, an owner who wants to leave the business (or force out another owner) may end up losing his or her investment or having to sue to dissolve the business to get out. It's not like selling off some shares on the stock market. The impact of not having things spelled out in an agreement can have devastating effects.

Growing Up in the Business

Family is the foundation of our society. Children are our inheritance, and children are greatly impacted by the family business. The impact can be both positive and negative.

One business owner I interviewed did not want his children to even consider running the family business, which had been in the family for two generations. He considered the work, the reward and the future to be so negative that he didn't want that for his kids. He had grown the business to include more than 30 employees and earn revenue of more than $3 million. He had subsequently shrunk it back after not having the management style and structure to manage the team. He ended up with four or five people working for him, and although the last chapter in this story hasn't yet been written, with his attitude I would be surprised if he were able to sell the business for even close to what it could be worth, thus affecting his retirement. With that type of attitude and perspective, do you think the next generation in his family will take the risk to own a business?

On the other hand, I see quite a few families that have done a great job at including their kids in the business. They get a job as a teen and have the opportunity to learn the business from the bottom up. They see the bond the family has and thrive on that opportunity. One specific example is a family business that the parents started and are still working in. All four of their children are also in the business. Two of them have been involved for two to three decades and a third joined due to personal circumstances. This allowed her a safe place to work, learn and succeed. She has done a fantastic job and brought to the family a set of skills and outside perspective that was very beneficial. The fourth child—who happens to be the youngest and the only male child—had no intention of being involved in the business. He worked in another city in another business and consistently indicated no interest in his family's business. His situation changed, however, and he was no longer employed. His interest in the family business also changed and he has become a vital member of the business.

Adding another family member has changed the dynamics of the family business. Some of the childhood challenges, rivalries and interactions have come into play. The next chapter in this story has also not been written. Will the family member who spent decades in the family business get her desired role of president/CEO upon the passing of her parents, or will the dynamics of having the only son in the business change that?

Both of these stories point out the challenges. As business owners, provide perspective for your children. Not all business is as hard as the first example. Teach your kids to evolve. How we do business today is very different from 100 years ago. There are industries like buggy manufacturing that have gone out of business; others have adapted and become stronger in the process. Show your children how to adapt. Show them your humanness by discussing what you have done wrong and how you would do it differently today.

So often I hear the owners of the business indicate that they want the business to be passed on to their children. That concept is fantastic—when it works. However, it takes much effort to make that happen. Often what I have seen is the children want no part of the business. They haven't seen the joys of business ownership; all they have seen is the work, long hours, frustration and their parents spending a huge amount of time away from home. If your vision really is to pass the business to your children, there are several considerations.

Spend time from an early age teaching them business—not *your* business but business in general. Teach them how to budget. Teach them about cash flow and how it affects decisions within the business. Teach them the basics of marketing and advertising. The lessons need to be age appropriate, but there are many ways to teach those basics even to 5- and 6-year-olds.

When my son received birthday and Christmas money when he was young, he wasn't allowed to spend it all. Although we had taught him the basics, he made decisions about how much to put in each "bucket": tithe/charity, short-term savings, long-term savings, his first house and retirement. What was left is what he had to spend on what he wanted, and he always had enough left over to do so. It truly isn't the amount put in each of those buckets; it was the habit and the education, and it is never too soon or too late to start the education process.

When he was preparing to get his driver's license, he had to pay for his car insurance. The entire year's worth of car insurance had to be in the bank before he could get his license or a car. Again, this wasn't about the money but about learning to save, not paying interest due to lack of planning or savings and having the money saved so he didn't get caught being unable to make a payment. He has learned those lessons well.

Spend time with your child in the fun part of the business. If you can't find a part of the business that is fun, you need to reconsider why you would saddle them with a business that isn't fun. Life is too short to not enjoy what you are doing. You probably want more for them. If you can't find a fun part of your business, step back and get someone—like a business coach—to help you take a closer look at your business, what you are doing and why you are doing it, and recapture the passion. Otherwise, you might lose it all—the family, the business and the ability to pass it on. This is preventable and not necessary, so take action.

Don't pressure your children to go into the business. That can cause them to run the opposite direction and never return, especially when they are teens. I often see parents wanting to live out their own dreams through their children. Although this is most common in sports, it also happens a great deal in business. Parents should not place their own dreams and goals on their children.

One business I worked with for a short while involved a couple who had purchased a franchise in their later years. Their goal was to pass the business to their children, especially the sons (the daughter didn't even pretend to be interested). The unfortunate side is the son who was to be the leader had no initiative and no desire to be the leader. He came to work every day and did what he was told, but without a complete change in attitude and initiative he would fail at running the business if it really were left to him. The parents were aware of his attitude and constantly discussed it, yet did nothing to truly ensure the son was prepared for what the future might bring.

One level of preparation might be firing him and forcing him to find work outside the family business. That may sound harsh to some of you (and probably not to others), but the choices are often to force the child to grow up and see the real world or continue to support him in the lifestyle to which he is accustomed and then allow him to fail at the family business. The challenge for every parent is to balance encouragement and challenge with forcing the child into something they don't desire, are not skilled at and makes them miserable. Tread carefully—it can affect your legacy.

Allow or require the child to go out and work for someone else at some point. Those lessons on how to get a job, how to keep it, and what it is like to not be related to the owner and have the associated privileges can be the greatest business lesson you will ever teach them. They need to learn how to work with other employees. They need to learn what it is like to be fired or laid off or asked to do something they don't want to do. They need to learn to stick with a job on the bad days. They will come back into the business being a far better business owner, manager and leader.

Make sure the business is one in which the child has some level of interest. One of my friends had a pool business and four sons. The oldest three worked in the business and had no passion to stay in it. There were other hills to climb, other challenges ahead of them. However, the fourth from a very young age knew he wanted to join the business when he grew up. In fact, he couldn't understand why he needed to finish school (he was in elementary school at the time). He knew he would work in the business and school was not something he cared about. His parents were wise and kept him focused on completing school and encouraged his passion to learn as much as possible about the pool business. Will he be successful? I believe he will be, even though he is currently in high school. He knows what he wants and has wise parents who are training him not only on how to service and install pools but also on what is really the most important part—running a pool business. I predict the family business won't be the only business he will run during his lifetime. Now that is a legacy to pass along to your kids.

COACH'S CORNER
Hiring Kids to Work in the Business

- Don't pay kids (or other family members) more than other employees, but do pay the market rate; otherwise, you will get resentment from the rest of the employees and other family members.
- Be willing to terminate the kids, just like you would any employee.
- Hire your child for an after-school or summer job. It is a way for them to get their feet wet and to better understand what their parents do all day, as well as provide an introduction to another side of business ownership.
- If at all possible, don't have the kids report to the parents. Do have them work with someone else in the business. Do give that person the power, right and responsibility to treat your child like any other employee. That means they can hold your child accountable for showing up on time, doing quality work and being responsible for completing their tasks. Make sure your child knows that their manager has those rights.

When I first started my business, my son was in sixth grade and I needed someone to handle the customer/prospect database I was building. I picked up around 500 business cards in the first three months through networking and had no desire to enter this information myself. My son was hired and paid a wage to do the work. Now I didn't have anyone else to manage him, so he did have to report to me. However, the conversation with him covered the rules of the game of how this relationship would work. One: I will always be your mom. Two: While you are doing work for me I am first your employer. That means what I say goes even if you don't like it. Three: You will do quality work, on time and with no attitude (we were just starting the teen years). Four: I have the ability to fire you and will if the above items are not handled. For us it worked.

There were times that schoolwork got in the way, but the rule was that school came first. He did this job for about three years and at around age 15 actually quit on me. He didn't enjoy the work any longer. It was sort of a relief for me. I was ready to replace much of what he did with technology. I had moved into an office and the practical side of what he did was no longer working. He also learned valuable lessons on work, quality and what he *didn't* want to do when he grew up—and that was a great lesson. Now he is back working for me using the technology and keeping up with what needs to be done.

One of the greatest parts about being the child of a business owner is the ability to get real-world experience in a job without the hassle of interviewing and competing with everyone else to get hired. One of the greatest downsides of being the child of a business owner is you are often expected to work in the business even if you don't like it, don't care about it and want to work elsewhere.

Thousands of books can be written on the impact of the family-owned business on the owner's children. My intent is not to address all the challenges or opportunities but to provide some basic recommendations.

The opportunities include:

- An ability to get real-life job experience in a relatively safe and supportive environment. Children can see what customers are all about and find out that while they aren't always nice, most of them are. Children can learn self-control, diplomacy, a strong work ethic and many other valuable lessons.
- An ability to work with their parents. This allows them to see the parents in a very different world—a world where they deal with pressure and customers and exhibit skills that may not necessarily

be seen at home. Kids can see how the parents handle conflict and negotiations. They learn what respect really means, how fast you can lose it and how hard it is to earn.

+ The opportunity to earn a paycheck and create independence.
+ The firsthand knowledge of how a business really operates.

Almost every opportunity listed above can be seen as a downside as well. For example, sometimes the family business isn't doing well financially, so the child essentially becomes slave labor. Additionally, they may learn all the negative sides of the business and not how to handle people, situations or themselves. Other negatives include:

+ Damage to their emotional well-being. Either the family or the non-family employees can contribute to this. Family members are not always welcomed into the business. Also, there can be almost a bullying attitude, either toward the child or from the child. Children often have no hesitation in bullying other employees if they think it will gain them something. They have usually learned these lessons at home.
+ Physical strain. Not all family businesses are easy and inside. If you are in the trades or do other outside work, the physical toll can be great.
+ Psychological damage. The stress of the business, if not handled well, can impact everyone's self-confidence. The failure of the business or individual activities can also have a long-lasting impact on everyone involved.

Many of the families I have worked with and interviewed have great relationships with their children and vice versa. Many of the kids (who are now adults with families of their own) saw the business as a blessing. Their identity as kids was often tied to the business. They learned responsibility, sacrifice, selling and numerous life lessons that take many adults decades to learn. Almost all of them worked outside the business for a period of time, which gave them an appreciation for the benefits of being in a family business. They appreciated the flexibility, growth and legacy that came with it. They also understood that no matter how old they are now, as long as the parents were involved in the business, they were still at times their parents' babies. That could involve the protective atmosphere that comes with protecting babies and can often be stifling. It often means that no matter how old you are, you still don't get your own way if your parents are involved in the business.

There is no perfect world, but often children who have grown up in a business and worked there, then stepped outside to see another world come back and settle in to what is a very wonderful and comfortable life of being the second- or third-generation business owners, and they hope their kids do the same.

Siblings and Extended Family in the Business

The dynamics of working with your siblings or having the owners' extended family in the family business can be simple and yet complicated. Much of the dynamic depends on the roles they play in the business and the relationship to the other family members. For example, if the owners' siblings are involved as employees, the dynamic can be fairly simple: They are simply an employee who just happens to work for their brother or sister. In an environment where the business is well run, there is accountability for quality of work and a business relationship is maintained, this situation can and does work well. Allow drama into the environment and all that hard work of building a business can be put at risk.

Family members who have little or no transactional ownership (i.e., no stock or financial ownership) should be treated the same way as non-family employees. There should be no difference between family and non-family members. Either treat everyone as family or treat everyone as employees. (I recommend the second option.) Consistency is really the key here. Promotions should be open to everyone. Bonuses, profit-sharing and pay increases should be handled the same for everyone. One very quick way to foster conflict and decrease morale among employees is to treat family members one way and non-family members another. This also pertains to increased responsibility and a career path. However, if non-family members will never be considered for a promotion or the executive ranks within an organization, then be up front with the potential employee from the beginning.

In one business I worked with the operations manager had been with the company for almost 25 years and saw potential for becoming a part owner and/or president. It was not anticipated that the son would show an interest in running the business since his two older siblings had not had any involvement. However, after 20 years, the youngest son decided he did want to work in the business. Because it had not been spelled out clearly from the beginning, there was a level of resentment and frustration from the operations manager. The reality was that there was never an option of him becoming a part owner. It will never be known if the operations manager just thought and dreamed of the possibility or if the owner had indicated the potential. In either case, the business owner had not been clear in an effort to avoid the situation. He had been aware of the desires of the operations manager but chose to ignore the potential issues. What it did create is animosity toward the son and next generation of management. Ignoring your problems usually does come back to bite you. I empathized with the operations manager as he realized that his potential for ownership and the executive role were dashed after all these years. Yet clarity on his part could have cleared things up many years ago. So for employees reading this, there is ownership on your part to ask as well. Don't assume; you know what assume means!

Working with your siblings can be an entirely different matter. If the owners left one sibling in charge when all of them have been working in the business for years, there can be rivalry. There is also the fact that because the siblings grew up together, they know how to push each others' buttons. Here are some other disadvantages to the sibling-owned environment:

Disadvantages of the sibling owned environment

+ The fights that took place when you were 12 (Mom always liked you better) and weren't resolved rear their ugly head in the workplace when least expected.
+ Family drama plays out on a continual basis if allowed
+ Siblings can take sides with one parent or another during disputes causing additional family grief "You always side with your Dad!"

Now for the advantages of the sibling-owned environment:
+ You can be direct because you know how your siblings think.
+ You are all in it together. That boat must stay afloat or the whole family sinks.
+ You understand each other. That doesn't mean you always agree, but you do understand.
+ You have a common bond, which often means a common work ethic and common values.

For extended family and siblings you have a choice. To make it work, to work harder on the sibling relationships than you do on the employee relationships and create the value, bond and leverage that comes from a successful family business. It will mean walking away from arguments and disagreements at work and picking your battles. Decide which battles you can compromise on and which you can't or won't. For example, what types of napkins you use for customers is not worth the fight, yet the culture of the business and the employee treatment might be worth having a stronger battle. At our office—not it isn't a family business, early on we decided which way the toilet paper would roll. Wasn't a big deal, but I have seen fights over less. It was a vote 4 out of 5 of us agreed. It sounds funny (and we do joke about it), and yet it allows us to come to agreement on the small stuff and move on to what is truly important.

Transitioning Family Members out of the Business

You have tried everything, yet reality is a family member either doesn't belong in the business, isn't qualified or just needs to leave the family business. Can it be done? Yes. Is it hard—absolutely. Is there an easy way—probably not, but it often must be done.

After you have tried all the avenues possible, sometimes a parting of the ways must happen. A family member must leave the business. How do you make it happen?

1. **Create a plan.** I have had husbands, wives, children all leave the family business because it was time. In every case, they ended up transitioning to new opportunities that fit their needs better than staying in the business. A transition plan is essential, especially if they have critical roles in the business. Sometimes that transition plan is short, sometimes it will take months. In either case it must be communicated and communicatead clearly.

2. **Be sensitive:** Unless there is a cause of illegal activity there should be no shame in leaving the business and the balance of the family should not indicate otherwise.

3. **Help** the departing family member with finding new opportunities. They must find what they want, but providing references, making connections, helping to strategize must be part of the plan

4. **Be firm:** Once you have decided they must leave (or they decided to leave) stick to the plan. Extending departure dates out weeks and months only leaves the family and the business in limbo

5. **Be honest:** Why do they need to leave? Is it a relationship issue? Productivity, quality of work, attention to detail? I am aware of a business that did transition out one of the founders in the business. He had lost his passion, was burned out, tired of the business and not able to perform his duties. His mindset and abilities was hampering the business in their ability to grow since he

held a critical role. The change had to take place, or the business would cease to exist.

6. **Be open:** Just because a family member had one role in a company doesn't mean they can't do something else—if they want to work in a different capacity. A husband and wife business was growing quickly. They had lots of opportunity. They had an exit strategy for the business. Then one day she realized that her husband was not respecting the rules, roles and desires they had both set out for the business. He was compromising what she believed were her standards. As a result she stepped down from her role in marketing to another role within the business that allowed her to help, keep her dignity and allow her husband to move the business forward. She could have left, but the family business allowed her the flexibility she would not get elsewhere so she chose to step aside.

It isn't easy to transition a family member out of the business, but it is possible and usually once it happens the family, the business and the employees all benefit from the transition.

CHAPTER **13**

Communication

Clear communication is important in any business but becomes especially important in the family business. Because poor communication can result in family rifts, it is essential that everyone learn to interact in a positive manner.

Guilt in the Family Business

There are families that do not build a foundation on guilt. I was fortunate to be part of such a family. We (or at least I) didn't do things based on guilt. Yes, there were obligations at times, yet the foundation for why we did things wasn't because of negative reinforcement, which is often where guilt comes in. One client I worked with guilted everyone across the board. If a decision did not match with what Mom wanted or felt was right, everyone in the family knew about it and guilt was poured on. This happened to the extent that family members were not allowed at the extended family table until enough time had passed or forgiveness had been granted. Although guilt is sometimes understandable in a setting that is strictly family, it has no place in the family business.

There is no greater guilt than what can be placed on those involved in family-owned businesses. The guilt comes from staying in the business or exiting the business. Working hard or not working hard enough. Guilt also comes from knowing that the family fortunes rise and fall on the success or lack thereof in the business. Guilt will not grow the business or build a solid foundation for the family that will transition a business from one generation to another. In fact, it can often destroy the business instead. However, wanting what is right for each family member and ensuring there is a path for each person in the business will help.

Build on the strengths that bind the family.

The opportunity here is the ability to step back and really understand the strengths of each person. Build on the strengths that bind the family. Recognize that the gifts of one family member are probably different from those of another. One may have the gift of detail, another has the gift of gab (aka selling), another may be the visionary and another has a practical financial side. Sometimes individuals have multiple gifts. No matter what the gift, understand it, explore it, exploit it; the end result is a benefit to the family, employees, customers and community.

Do You Hear What I Hear? Adapting Your Communication

Does everyone think the way you do? Obviously not, or the world would be a pretty boring place. You know your children each have their own individual personalities and what motivates one doesn't motivate another. That same concept is true with your customers, your parents and your spouse. So how do you handle the different personalities that you encounter and how does that impact the relationships within the family? There are many different personality profile tools on the market, all of which essentially provide the same types of information. They help you understand more about yourself and about those you encounter. These tools can be valuable in helping you to better understand how to motivate, encourage, hold accountable and praise the people you work with.

One of my favorite tools is called DISC, which stands for Dominant, Influencer, Steady and Conscientious, as detailed below:

+ D's are **dominant** individuals. They make decisions quickly, tend to look at things at a summary level and have a short attention span.
+ I's are **influencers**. They are the party animals and are always looking to have people around them. They organize the office party and often keep the team together and speaking with one another.
+ S's are **steady**. They want things predictable, stable and known. They are reliable, dependable and conscientious.
+ C's are **conscientious**. They do what you say, like detail, want things to be proven, and want to know what is going to happen when and how it will impact them.

Often people have a mix of the behavioral types. For example, you can have the "SC" behavior style, where a person wants the detail, and wants to know what will happen, how it will happen and the resulting impact. If they are communicating with a high "D," who after the first two sentences is off thinking about something else and just wants the bottom-line summary, what do you think the end result is of the encounter?

My profile is a high D and I, which means I am highly social and a very quick decision maker. My husband, however, has no D or I in his profile. He therefore is slower to make decisions, likes to investigate things at a high level of detail and doesn't like lots of change in short periods of time. He wants things orderly and wants the full picture before he makes a decision.

We have a TV that is under warranty and breaks. It can't be fixed, so we receive money to replace the TV. Now if it were up to me, I would go out and look at possibly two stores, pick the TV that I like and take it home that day, install it and be done. My husband, on the other hand, researches on the Internet, visits five stores, and does a comparison between the reliability, features and pricing of various brands. This takes probably three months (we weren't in a hurry since the other TV still worked even though it had issues). I finally just said, go do the research and let me know what you think are the top 2. He did just that. The decision was made and the TV is wonderful.

I am able to let him do his thing because I understand his personality profile. It was an eye-opener when we did the behavior profiles. I determined he really wasn't trying to be a pain; it was just who he was and that was part of what I loved about him (at least most of the time).

We have worked this out and it doesn't create conflict, yet what I see in business owners is that this type of process creates high levels of stress and frustration. One person analyzes things to death and won't make a decision. The other person makes decisions too quickly without the analysis, and it costs the business money and opportunities. Both situations can cost the business and create stress. In our situation, if we needed that TV quickly, I would have stepped in and hurried the process. It wasn't necessary, so why create the stress? If the Super Bowl had been the next week, however, the process would have gone much faster!

Knowing and understanding the behavioral types of family members can help you build on their strengths. So often people get pushed into areas that are not their strengths and are not given the training and knowledge they need to compensate. If someone is detail oriented, then allow them to do the research, yet understand they can research things to death before making a decision. An engineer spent so much time deciding what new car to purchase that the new model year was out and the desired car was no longer available. Note that too much research can create missed opportunities.

That is why the balance between the detail-oriented individual (the SC in DISC) and the D is critical. The D will make the decisions to get things moving and adjust quickly as needed, while the SC will provide the detail the D needs to make the best decisions. Therefore, if you are business owners and are both S or C, then you need to compensate with a D who will force decisions to be made. On the other hand, if you are a D and your spouse is an I, someone needs to do the research to ensure the business will survive. Without balance, the financial impact can be catastrophic.

Conflict

Conflict is part of everyday life. If you have a business, marriage or relationship without conflict, then you essentially are a yes man, which means you acquiesce even if you don't agree, simply to avoid conflict—which is in and of itself conflict. I would recommend every business owner take a mediation or conflict resolution class. There are numerous books on the subject, including *Getting to Yes: Negotiating Agreement Without Giving In* by Roger Fisher, William L. Ury, and Bruce Patton. The sooner you learn how to deal with conflict, the better off life will be.

One of my clients was engaged. Life was sweet for both of them. They enjoyed being together, they were obviously in love with each other, yet trouble was brewing. Every time he wanted something and she disagreed, she caved in. This was very evident in the business environment. It had been his business. She was new to his business, yet

> *The sooner you learn how to deal with conflict, the better off life will be.*

was very accomplished on her own and actually has better business sense than he does. Yet every time she suggested something and he disagreed, she would back down, both in business and in their personal lives. He even started wondering when she was going to stop being so agreeable. It will happen and for both of them it will be a rude awakening as neither had really learned how to negotiate. They hadn't learned the art of give and take and how to move both their ideas forward without squelching the spirit of the other person.

Another set of clients were partners. They both had their strengths in the business but again had never learned to look past the idiosyncrasies of their partners. Statements would be made and one or the other would take it the wrong way. Eventually one of the partners bought out the other just to reduce the conflict in their lives and to hopefully remain friends, which was becoming very difficult.

These examples are no different from any other marriage or business. It has been said that business relationships and marriage are never 50/50. Rather they are 100/100. Each person must give 100 percent in what they are doing and must try to always give 100 percent. We will never achieve 100 percent all the time, but our partner is able to pick up the pieces when we can't. With that attitude, the business and marriage will not only survive but will thrive.

That survival concept is one I want to touch on. Many reading this book may have the perspective of "We are surviving. We are making it." My question is where are you settling? Surviving is not good enough; I want to thrive in what I do, how I serve and what I contribute to my world. What about you? Is surviving all you want? What will it take to truly thrive in your business and your personal life?

I recently attended a conference where the speaker was discussing conflict. She pointed out four ways people react to conflict and how to change that behavior:

1. The exploder who blames others. This is the person who the moment conflict arises essentially explodes and reacts to the situation. Step back and learn how to address the issue without attacking the person.

2. The exploder who shame themselves. This is a person who by exploding essentially makes a fool of themselves in the process. They then get down on themselves for how they reacted, which makes things worse. Instead, stop, look around and ask yourself this question: If this is the worst thing that happens to me today, isn't it still a pretty good day?

3. The stuffer who builds barriers. This is the person who when asked how their day is say, "I'm fine!" even when that is the furthest thing from the truth. They build barriers, shutting down communication and therefore any intimacy in the relationship. It is OK to build a boundary—not a barrier—but you must keep talking. Not talking in a family business affects not only the family but also the business, customers, employees and long-term relationships.

In a relationship, you can either be right or be improving the relationship.

4. The person who collects "retaliation rocks." This is the person who has to prove something all the time. They are right; you are wrong. They always have something they can throw at you, something to hold over your head to ensure they have the ammunition to prove they are accurate (at least in their mind). In a relationship, you can either be right or be improving the relationship; you can't do both at the same time. It is your choice.

Realize that conflict is universal—we all face it. Conflict happens when we feel exposed or we feel imposed upon. However, our feelings are indicators, not dictators, of how we should act and react to conflict. Knowing how to handle it is critical.
Designing a business relationship that has a positive focus on conflict resolution has four critical points.

1. Do not confuse good relations with approval.
   You may get along with and like the other person, but you don't necessarily approve of what they are doing. Yet if you don't have ground rules for discussion and ensuring approval, actions can and will take place that will generate conflict.
2. Do not be confused by the roles of shared values.
   You and the other person may have shared values, but that does not mean you are going to agree with them all the time. The

COACH'S CORNER
Conflict Resolution

Here are some ideas for alleviating conflict:

- Role reversal: Try taking the other person's perspective and negotiate the points from that perspective. If done correctly and objectively, this exercise can open up your perspective to areas you aren't considering.

- Step away from the conflict. Go for a walk to clear your head before you say something you don't really mean (or something you do mean but should not be said). Working alongside a family member all the time can create a higher level of stress due to things that are unsaid. Often non-family employees will say things and clear the air much faster—they have less to lose.

- Separate the people from the problem. If you were to step back and understand the conflict as not with the individual but as the conflict itself, you can be far more objective in the potential resolution.

- Be as objective as possible and understand both what you want out of the resolution and what the other party would like. If you are always looking for a win for you and not for the other party, it is doubtful the resolution will be positive.

- Stop avoiding the discussions that lead to conflicts. Fear prevents people from discussing uncomfortable topics. That fear of conflict actually leads to much greater conflicts. If the discussion takes place prior to escalation, the discussion can be much more objective.

- Determine when starting the business how you will address conflict at work. That may be much different from how you address conflict at home. If the family tendency is to avoid conflict, make sure you have someone else whom you like and trust to help mediate. Third parties are great in these situations. If not, life and business will be full of unresolved conflict, and seldom does the individual or the business flourish in this environment.

best example is child rearing. Two people may have a shared value of not having spoiled children, but they may take different paths to reach that goal. Another example is having a shared value of excellent customer service but each person defines that customer service very differently.

3. Do not make avoiding disagreement an objective.

There will always be disagreement, especially in family businesses where often decades of behavior, both overt and covert, have shaped the family environment. Often not talking about things is the foundation of why the family gets along.

One of my clients was a very successful multigenerational business that had that type of undercurrent within the organization and family: Don't confront Mom; it isn't worth it. Mom wasn't open to new ways of doing things and avoided confrontation both within the family and with non-family employees. The end result was a high level of turnover within the organization that the parents just attributed to people changing jobs. The reality is the environment within the organization was essentially toxic and people could handle the situation for only so long. That environment won't change until the parents retire and the next generation is able to hopefully fix the work situation. The question will then become whether they have lived with it for so long that they will no longer be able to make the change. Time will tell.

4. Do not treat either side as "fixed" in a discussion.

We all change our minds. If someone is fixed in their opinions all the time, then that is a completely different discussion. Given logical, objective reasoning and positive, structured discussion, perspectives can be changed. Create a set of ground rules within the family to allow for this type of discussion; your stress level will thank you.

Frank started a business with his brother back in the 1970s. One had passion and the other needed a job, but both were too young to fully understand the implications of what would take place. The business thrived, yet one of the brothers wasn't pulling his full weight. I have only gotten one side of the story, but it is too familiar to not have elements of truth. Facts in some respect don't make a difference because the net result is two brothers who no longer speak to each other and a generation of brothers fractured. They started the endeavor with two different sets of perspectives, passions and goals. What is the moral to this part of the story? When you start a business between siblings, make sure you have identified the roles, responsibilities and passions of each. Define who is to do what. Create a firmly defined process for handling grievances. That did not happen in this story, or the brothers wouldn't be in the situation where they are not speaking to each other. Truth be told, families like these split even when there isn't a business involved, but the moment money and control become involved the stakes in the game rise exponentially.

Now let's fast forward to the next generation—the sons of one of the business's founders. Again, two brothers became involved in the business. Both are now in their 20s. One is no longer involved and they no longer speak to each other or have a relationship. One had a passion for the business and the other had not yet found his passion, but it was obviously *not* the family business. This has significantly strained the family relationship.

Here is an interesting observation: When I asked the dad questions about the effect on the family, although he did not diminish the emotional strain, he did indicate that if he had the choice to start the business again he would do it with no question. When I asked the same question of the mom, the answer was no, not because of the business but because of the effect it has had on family relationships. The business wasn't worth the result of damaged family relationships.

The business owners at this point (husband/wife) do have a good relationship with each other. They have learned to weather the storms of life, business, family and relationships and have grown stronger. Their recommendations for you are:

* **Communicate:** Communication is critical. Do it often and continually. The little things can and will get in the way. Figure out how to move through them. This couple spoke on the way home even though they didn't drive together. They addressed issues from work while on the phone with each other. One advantage this provided was that neither could see the other's body language. That helped by keeping out subtle (and not-so-subtle) signals such as eye rolling, crossed arms and other body language. By the time they got home (and they had a 45-minute commute), everything was addressed and they shut off *all* business discussion. It was now time for family, personal and everything other than business.

* **Set boundaries:** When they started the business, they did not establish boundaries and conflict arose. So they stopped and defined those boundaries, sort of like job descriptions: Who does what? What are the responsibilities? Who is in charge of what area? Once the boundaries were established, each stepped away from the other's areas. If one was to do invoicing, then that person had the final say in invoicing. If one was managing the field staff, the other spouse did not get involved with that aspect of the business. This also prevented the team from playing one against the other. Team members can often be like children and play one manager, owner or family member against another if allowed to.

* **Be aware of the little things:** The old saying about "the straw that broke the camel's back" can be very true in the family business. Little things create friction among the family. These include:

* **Pulling rank.** Having one family member pull rank in front of the team is enough to create a high level of friction. It demoralizes the chastised family member, disrespects them and shows the team how to create a wedge between family members. Long and short— don't do it. If rank needs to be pulled, revisit the boundaries you drew up and redefine them. If rank still needs to be pulled, do it in private—not in front of the whole team. Then determine how to prevent this situation from ever happening again.

Jack owns a business. His son, Steve, has worked in the business for a few years and is learning how to manage the team. Steve decides to implement a new process with the team he manages, but the team doesn't really like the new process so they complain to Jack. Jack doesn't like the new process either because it's never been done that way before. Jack then tells Steve's team that he will "take care of it." There are two mistakes here: 1) Steve should have gotten Jack's input before making policy or procedural changes. This is true in all companies simply to eliminate this type of situation. 2) Jack should have gone to Steve with the goal of understanding all the reasons for the change and either allowed the new process to succeed or fail on its own or challenged Steve to revert to the old process if the new one isn't in the best interest of the business. To "take care of it" just creates division between Dad and son and between Steve and his team—creating another time waste in the business.

- Treating your spouse as "one of the guys." For some wives, this can be OK. For others, this is a good way to sleep on the couch permanently. Your wife is not one of the guys. Don't treat her that way. She wants things to be different with you. She wants to be treated special, even at work. She may work with you, but she is still your wife. Don't take her for granted.
- Disagreeing about employees. Two different perspectives often arise regarding employees. One sees value in the person; the other wants them out of the business. This is actually easily solved with measurable performance evaluations. If the person is truly doing their job, meeting their goals and fulfilling their roles, there's no reason to get rid of them. However, very seldom do I see this in action. What usually happens is the employee isn't given measureable goals and the fuzzy part of work takes over. They are good at some parts of their job but not other parts. The husband likes how they deal with clients; the wife is constantly frustrated by the lack of paperwork like invoicing information that doesn't get filled out, which causes delays in billing and the resulting cash collection. This

disagreement creates grief for all parties and discord between the husband and wife and between them and the employee.

To prevent this situation, provide roles and responsibilities and have measurable and objective ways to determine if team members are performing their job. What is stopping them from achieving the objectives? Does the individual need additional tools or training to be effective in the job? A business owner had a valued employee who was not performing up to the standard he required, but he believed she had the skills. He invested in her with coaching and training to provide her the tools she needed to perform the job. She was then able to step up and accomplish her tasks, saving the company an employee and the cost and hassle of replacing her.

COACH'S CORNER
Learn to Laugh

Business and life are sometimes best handled with humor. Bad things will happen. Situations will arise that will take away your momentum, sometimes your dreams, and your passions. As the old song goes: Pick yourself, dust yourself off and start all over again. The only other option would be to run away screaming. When it is a family business, the challenges can impact your peace of mind.

Perspectives:
+ Learn to laugh at yourself—Life will be more fun
+ Learn to laugh with others—You share so much more when you laugh with others
+ Learn how to take a bad situation and find the good. There is good in everything if you look for it
+ Time may not allow you to heal without a scar, nor forget, but if you allow, time will return your desire to small laugh and enjoy life.

CHAPTER 14

Boundaries

Georg loved his business. He had attended school for many years to become a good doctor, was good at medicine and followed in his family footsteps. After a number of years of hiring out the administration part of his practice, he and his wife, Katie, decided to have her become involved in the operation. She was good at working with patients, completing the administrative tasks and helping in all the ways possible. Both George and Katie were busy all day long and didn't take time during the day to discuss business matters.

As all business owners know, it is the little things that can be the difference between peace and frustration in the daily life of business. Yet it is the little things that often don't get addressed until they are no longer little things.

Katie wanted to start regular weekly meetings with George to discuss the business and often tried to have these discussions once they both arrived at home. George, however, did a great job (better than most) of leaving business at the office once he walked out the door. Katie figured, what better time than during the evening after dinner when the kids were doing their homework or engaging in other activities to have the office discussions. The result was friction as they both dug in their heels.

Fortunately for them, after a few months of back-and-forth discussion, they came to an agreement to go out to lunch every other week, just the two of them, to discuss business. This allowed George and Katie to address business issues during the day and enabled them to grow their business.

Boundaries are probably the most important aspect of running a successful family business without destroying relationships. It doesn't ensure one or both parties won't overstep the boundaries, but at least they are drawn. Boundaries are required in many areas, including between home and work, among roles within the business and between family members and employees.

Home to Work, Work to Home

Establish early on, or *now* if you are already in business, how you want to operate. One couple who owned a business had a routine of talking about any issues, challenges and opportunities during their drive home, either together or separately. However, when they walked through the door, their focus was on the family, and no business was discussed. I loved one of the wife's comments: "I often went home from the office earlier than my husband. He would

Look forward to his arrival home and the transition from business owners to a family.

call me on the way home and we would discuss the day. This allowed me to have a conversation with him, without his seeing the look on my face and my body language. This freedom allowed me to shake it off, get it out and move on. Our commute was about a half hour so it was a good time to be productive. This also allowed me to look forward to his arrival home and the transition from business owners to a family."

That type of boundary system may not work for everyone. It did for them, and 40 years of marriage was the testament to that fact. The important aspect is they created a boundary. They created a process for communicating that worked. What is your process?

Roles Outside the Family

Business relationships are a lot like families—even when you aren't related. Children will play one parent against another unless boundaries are set. If boundaries aren't set for the kids, then that third cookie, or the 1a.m. curfew will become a tension point with the parents. "But I told him he couldn't have the third cookie. Why did you say yes?" "I didn't know you had said no." Sound familiar? In our household the first question was: "Have you asked your dad about this?" If the answer was no, then I would provide a response. If the answer was yes, then my response was, "What did he say?" Actually that didn't happen very much as our son knew what would happen if he were caught playing us against each other. The consequences were much greater than he wanted to contend with. Boundaries had been established early on in his life.

This scenario plays out in all businesses, but especially in the family business where roles and responsibilities are not well defined. Mom is seen as the authoritarian decision maker in most areas, yet Dad has his very distinctive roles. However, when the employees don't like Dad's answer, they know Mom will often contradict what Dad has said. Trouble ensues. It might not at that moment or that day or even that month, but if this continually happens, confidence, respect, loyalty and business health go downhill.

These concepts are not limited to just employees. Suppliers, customers and partners will also push the envelope if the boundaries are not clear. Making an end run is a common tactic. The supplier knows that the president makes all the final decisions and is easy to get along with. The supplier also knows their contact hasn't returned calls and isn't

COACH'S CORNER

Roles and Responsibilites

- Each employee—family or not—must have his or her areas of responsibility that are defined clearly to everyone, both within the family and outside.

- When there is a disagreement between two parties, it should not be handled in front of the team (or customers, for that matter). When the resolution is defined, the person responsible for the specific area must be the one to address the change, thereby reestablishing their authority. The attitude in which the resolution is communicated is paramount. Should either party show anything but unified support, division and disintegration can occur.

- Successful family businesses usually do not combine the two environments. They work hard to keep things separate. Each party knows what is acceptable and what isn't and they stick to it as much as possible.

- Respect is absolutely critical for successful boundaries. You might not agree with what the other party wants for a boundary, but you must respect their desires. At least try the boundary; business is all about experimenting with new ideas and boundaries can be an area in which to experiment. One person may not like mornings; the other loves them but hates nights. Sit down and talk about it, and create flexibility where possible.

open to considering their new products. What is the process for how these situations are handled? Being a salesperson at heart myself, I have had countless conversations with my own sales teams regarding whether we should go over the head of our contact. There are risks and benefits to that decision; however, if not doing an end run around our contact means we lose the deal, then the risk outweighs the downside. (That is, we will lose the prospect if we don't go over their head, but if we tick them off by going to their boss, we may lose anyway. *But* we may win. The potential win is sometimes worth the risk.)

In a family business, not having a discussion about how these types of tactics will be handled can create drama that is not productive. That is not to say this doesn't happen in non-family businesses, but the emotion and downsides can be a bit greater in the family business. Determining up front how end runs will be addressed will save you time, energy and emotion, which will save you money.

PART FOUR

*Evolution of a
Family Business*

When you start your business, you're full of hopes and dreams. You have created a family business. And when it goes well, you'll run the business for decades. But what happens when you want out?

There can be many reasons for wanting out: You're ready to retire; your family isn't interested in continuing the business; your partner is no longer compatible or is unable to continue with the business for some reason; or your partner dies. Or perhaps you die. (Sorry, but reality must play into this discussion.)

Nobody likes to think about what happens when it's all over. But denial or fear is no reason to not plan. You must think of yourself, your business and your family. This part of the book addresses how you can do that through estate planning and transition plans. In addition, consider the legacy you want to leave.

CHAPTER 15

Wills and Estate Planning

Let's look at what could happen to Sean and Marsha's business if Marsha died suddenly. If they didn't plan ahead and have a shareholder agreement or operating agreement with terms about what happens when an owner (s) dies, Marsha's interest will pass to her heirs (who may or may not be the same as Sean's heirs). Marsha's heirs could include a spouse (if she and Sean are siblings, for example), child, other relative, a trust or foundation or some combination of these. Let's hope she at least has a will.

Even if a business owner does have a will, it's possible none of the heirs have any interest in working in the business or have the qualifications to do so if, for example, Marsha was a dentist or other licensed professional. But the heirs still have a right to Marsha's share of the profits and a say in the management. Whatever Marsha contributed to the business in terms of productivity, sales, service or cash is gone and the new owners may have unrealistic expectations about the inheritance they just received. This can especially be true if proper documents that spell out who gets what parts of the inheritance have not been drawn up.

Sean is faced with a quandary when his co-owner dies. Can he buy out the new owners? Does he want to buy out the new owners? Will the new owners sell? How much is the business worth? Can he continue operating the business alone? Even just to fulfill existing orders? And don't forget that Sean may have lost his spouse, so he's not his usual happy, clear-headed self.

It's not just death that causes issues business ownership issues. Divorce is a risk for small companies, particularly when both husband and wife are owners. The business is one more asset to divide (and fight about) in a divorce and may be the primary source of income of one or both spouses. Without an agreement about how an owner can exit the business, a divorce could destroy it.

Protecting Your Business

Stephen Covey coined the phrase: Begin with the end in Mind. If it wasn't done when the business was started, it's best to have these discussions in the early stages when the founders of the family business are still alive, healthy, friendly and cooperative. There should be no embarrassment about agreeing on a buyout clause or getting life insurance or other investments to cover the loss of a key member or fund a buyout. And if tragedy strikes—or life happens—a process is in place to manage the situation.

Here are a few basic questions to ask when thinking about the future of your business. It is not a complete list by any means. My recommendation is seek the advice of a lawyer. Don't try to become a lawyer and write a will by yourself off the Internet. You need to hire a professional to handle your will and estate plan. Any time you have a business, there are numerous complications and considerations that won't affect you if you aren't around, but will affect everyone left behind: your spouse, children, employees, vendors, bankers and the list goes on.

- Who will sign checks so employees are paid?
- Who will make sure the IRS is paid sales or employee taxes so the business isn't saddled with penalties? Note that the IRS doesn't accept excuses, so the fact that the heirs didn't know any taxes were due isn't an acceptable reason to not pay them.
- Who actually has ownership of the business now?
- Who will make basic decisions, like purchasing inventory, so the business can continue to operate and serve customers?
- If the owner had done the accounting themselves, then who is the backup who knows the books and can keep the financials accurate during this crisis?
- Who knows how to access:
  › credit card information to ensure payments are being made
  › bank accounts
  › social media accounts
- What is the process of managing cash to ensure all the bills are paid?

I have spoken to many business owners who own a business they really didn't want because no plans were laid out for when Dad passed away. Mom, who was not previously a part of the business, is now deeply involved but has no experience, no desire and no option other than to learn the hard way. This happens even when both are involved in the business. There isn't a backup plan. Mom knows her side of the business, but Dad's side was always a mystery and one she didn't care to know or understand. My recommendation in these businesses is to always do two things:

- Have documentation and systems in place that will allow others to step in and run the business. Many things can and should be documented, thereby allowing someone new to the business to step in, read the procedures and execute.

+ Know your heir apparent. This means you should always be training someone to take on various aspects of your job. There may not be the ability to train someone to do everything you do, but you can divide up your various roles and have others step up to do pieces.

For example, let's say Mom is the president of the company. She is the visionary and chief salesperson, and also handles customers and manages the finances. Mom may not be able to delegate and train someone to have vision—that may depend on the other employees— however, she can ensure there is another person who can step up and sell the products and services. In this case, Dad was the architect of the product so Mary, who helps with sales in conjunction with Dad, can keep the sales funnel moving and new customers coming in the door. It may take two people to do this job for a while until either someone is hired or Mary determines that she is not only good at sales but likes it!

Dealing with finances is much easier: Have a CPA on hand as your trusted advisor who, along with your bookkeeper, can manage the finances so the family will know the financial situation of the business essentially without missing a beat. Document where files, accounts and important papers are located and keep those materials current.

Harry owned a business. He handled all the finances but had a team that worked the retail side of the business. Harry had a stroke, and then a few weeks later he had a second stroke. He was now paralyzed on one side of his body and the chances of him returning to the business were slim. No one in his family wanted anything to do with the business unless they absolutely had to—and now they absolutely had to become involved. They wanted to close the business, but the business is what put food on the table for the family. Tension soared and stress increased.

The first thing course of action was a full accounting of the state of the business. What bills were outstanding? What cash was coming in? What was the cash flow? What was the debt load of the business. A plan needed to be put into place. Would they sell the business, could it operate on its own, could a manager be hired in. What would have made this entire process much easier is having a plan for what should take place if anything happened and having documentation to ensure others knew what to do. None of that was in place here, which just added to the family stress.

Would that happen for you? Who would run your business while you are out? Remember that in the family business, it is not only the family that is caught up in the unexpected but also the business. The answers to those questions can make the difference between survival and bankruptcy for the business. Thinking about what could happen and making a plan for the next steps in this type of crisis is a process that should be reviewed every year.

Talk to any lawyer and they will shake their head at the number of people who are in denial about the two facts of life: death and taxes.

In reality, the concept of being indispensable only feeds your ego. The true business owner spends most of their time making sure they are dispensable so that with or without them the business moves on and provides the value to the community, family and employees they set out to provide.

Protecting Yourself

Over and above the consideration of the business is my strong recommendation to have a will. Talk to any lawyer and they will shake their head at the number of people who are in denial about the two facts of life: death and taxes. Wills can impact both. One of my close friends passed away from an illness. Even though she and her husband had done some basic planning, her husband has become an advocate of planning even more thoroughly when it comes to death.

Here are a few basic guidelines on the personal side:

+ Make sure your spouse, attorney, CPA and a member of your advisory team such as business partners, executive management know where your will and other important documents are kept.

- Have a medical power of attorney. The laws change frequently so don't assume your family will have the access you think they do.
- Talk about The transition plan. What are your desires in the case of an accident, death or prolonged illness. The topic may be uncomfortable, but the discussion needs to happen.
- Don't leave any communication to memory. Write down who gets your grandmother's wedding ring that was passed down to you. Death brings out the worst in many families.

Bringing in an Outsider

When you add in a business, the chances of the process being simple and without drama are about the same as winning the lottery. One of the best things you can do is to have a non-relative on staff at a high level—someone that can be depended on to run the business while your family is focused on other issues.

"But she isn't family!" some family members may say. Two primary scenarios are at play here. One, someone who isn't family is hired to help run the company because that is what is best for the business. Two, someone is hired to run the company because no one else wants to or is qualified.

We have spent the last few chapters talking about what happens when the unexpected happens. One way to help mitigate the potential disaster awaiting the business is to have a non-family member involved in and knowledgeable about the operations of the business. This provides two benefits: The family can take a vacation, handle emergencies or be away for other reasons and someone else can run things. Additionally, the family gets an outside perspective on the business that isn't filtered through the family blinders. Both allow for balance in the business and provide a safety net for the family.

Often the situation presents itself that there are no family members who can adequately lead the business. The difference is the family recognizes the fact that none of them wants the leadership role or is adequately equipped to lead the business. The family must first agree that their strengths and passions are not in this activity. The roles could be varied, from sales or finance to president or chief product architect. The first step is the awareness; it truly starts with the vision for the company. What or who is holding back the growth? Is it one or more of the family members? In a husband/wife team, one or both of you may not be equipped to do all that needs to be done. You must recognize this fact and take the appropriate action.

There are countless examples of companies in which both spouses try to make a go of it with one or the other in the wrong position. It strains the marriage, the family and the children—even if the children are grown. For example, Jerry was the product and delivery champion. He did a great job, the customers were happy, and the potential to grow the business was significant. However, Amy, his wife, continually stood in the way of growth. Doing the books and networking overwhelmed her and she wasn't enjoying either; therefore, the family was feeling the strain. This company was almost out of business at the writing of this book. Jerry was unwilling to stand up to his wife (yes, I recognize this is very hard to do) and do what was right for the business and, I contend, what was right for the family as well.

Much of this comes back to getting out of comfort zones. Eleanor Roosevelt once said: "Do one thing every day that scares you." If you don't take that risk, you and your business will not grow. It is like not allowing a baby to try to walk or sit up or talk. Seldom does a baby just sit back and not try. They are always looking at the world in a new way. They want to reach out for that new thing or scoot across the room. Somewhere along the path to adulthood, many people lose their desire to stretch, grow and learn. That essentially becomes the beginning of death. If one or both spouses are not willing to step out of the comfort zone and look at the business in a different way, the prospects for true success grow faint.

One business I worked with had grown substantially and was (and still is) well respected in the community. A key employee was responsible for all the operations of a particular division. While I worked with the company. we uncovered all the things she *wasn't* doing. We put evidence together of her misdeeds—things like taking more than 40 days off during the year, requiring vendors to bring her things she liked (i.e., bribes), berating team members, etc. We really began to understand the impact this person had on the entire organization, not just her division.

When I arrived, I was essentially told this individual was untouchable and would never be let go. Now my purpose wasn't to get this person fired. My purpose was to educate the division executive whom I was coaching to improve profitability, team environment and leadership skills. The challenge became not proving what this employee needed to change (she was unwilling to see that any changes in her behavior were required), but to convince the business owner that the change was required. It took almost eight months to make the change and have her removed. The reason became obvious—this employee had become close friends with the business owner's wife. The pressure he received to *not* have this person fired impacted his judgment on what needed to be done.

The wife was somewhat involved in the business, and I believe this involvement cost the business tens of thousands of dollars—just during the time I coached. That doesn't take into account the previous years, the low employee morale, high turnover or frustration of vendors (who disliked working with her). The change was eventually made and I had team members emailing me and thanking me even months later for helping to make this happen. They had been miserable and hated going to work. They now saw the potential in the company and their role at the company. The moral of the story: Understand the impact your spouse can have on your decisions. Sometimes life at home can get rough, but stand tall, make sure you get the full picture and make the decisions that need to be made. Your business, your team, your customers and your vendors will thank you. Now that becomes a legacy.

For those who are family members and have grown up in the family business, here are some suggestions:

+ Require all family members to work for at least three years in other businesses or industries before they come to work for the family business. This is common business sense. Allow the family members to see what the real world is like. They can gain experience and appreciate the family business in a completely different way. Some businesses grant senior management a sabbatical to work in other areas outside their job or business roles. I would recommend that family businesses do the same. Once every 10 years, they need to volunteer in another business or a nonprofit organization in order to widen their perspective. I guarantee that process will open their eyes and improve the profitability of their own business.

+ Have a promotion path for non-family members. Nothing demotivates talented people faster than realizing they don't have a future in the organization—no career path, no promotions and essentially a cap on income. This pushes talented people out the door and often to the competition. Now if you want to remain small and don't want a career path for outsiders, that is fine. Then hire to that premise. Don't hire without the people knowing there is no upward growth past a certain level. In the long run, it will save you money as you won't need to continually replace personnel. Having to replace personnel is a profitability drain and won't help you build business value.

One business I worked with realized that most of their employees never stayed more than three or four years. They hired good people, but those people didn't stay long term. The owners chose not to grasp the concept that there was no career path, no place to grow and no investment in the staff, and therefore the staff chose to grow elsewhere. In this particular situation, the work environment was also fairly toxic. All non-family members were essentially afraid to tell the owners the issues with the business. The ones who did stay were essentially those who had looked but had not been able to find a job elsewhere or didn't have the drive to make the business better. They were there to get a paycheck. Is that what you want?

Educate the family and everyone else in the business on the basics of business. The more employees understand the basic tenets of business, the better chance they have of making decisions that will benefit the company, which essentially benefits the employee as well as the family members.

Passing Along the Passion

When a multigenerational family business continues to grow, the owners need to think about how they will manage the transition.

Mom and Dad started the business more than 30 years ago. Then decided at one point to move to another city and start the business again. That was more than 25 years ago. Their children have all become involved and now they are looking at the grandchildren starting to become involved. They have been very successful and have provided not only for their own family but also for the families of many employees. They have done so many things extraordinarily well. The fact that the family still enjoys each other's company, likes to be together and is encouraging the third generation to become involved is a statement to the nature of the business owners. The challenge is in truly turning over the reins of the business to the second generation. Times have changed, the needs of the family continue to change and what worked 20 years ago doesn't work in the same way today. They recognize the challenges ahead and I believe they are scared about how the transition will take place.

The upside: The community knew who they were, what they stood for and how important the business was to each of them. The grand-children had a sense of belonging, which actually became that check and balance for the parents. The kids knew if they did something wrong that someone was always around who knew their parents and grandparents. It taught them maturity, gave them a sense of grounding and made them who they are today.

There are essentially three ways to pass down a family business:

- **Be organized:** The parents pick an heir apparent, lay out the organization structure and spend the next five to 10 years grooming the new team and stepping out of the business more and more. They begin turning over the business to the new team. They let the kids start making decisions, knowing and understanding that mistakes will happen. After all, the parents made mistakes, too. They need to allow the kids to learn while providing a safety net of advice.

  › The challenge is in giving up control. I hear you now: "I would be thrilled to give up control of the business." Yes, you say that—until one of the new leaders makes a decision you don't like. I see it all the time (and this happens in all businesses). Leaders give up control until they don't like the decisions being made, then they step back in and take back control, and the resentment starts. The second-guessing and the lack of trust result in an unwillingness to try again.

  › Here is another factor: The kids are a perfect blend of the parents—warts and all. The things one doesn't really care for in the spouse manifest themselves in the kids. One is wild; the other is too conservative. One is visionary; the other wants things to be the same they have always been. The end result is parents who are afraid; everything they have worked toward for the last 30-plus years now has the potential of being a disaster, going out of business or otherwise changing. This fear can hold the business back and stunt its potential. This fear can be well-founded; however, if the parents feel the children do not have the skills to run a business, then a plan must be put in place to enable them to run the business or someone else needs to be placed in charge of the business to move it forward. Often that can be a relief to that next generation who either isn't skilled or doesn't want the responsibility of running the business. And that is OK; not everyone is gifted at the risk taking and responsibility of business ownership, but they will be skilled at other things.

+ **Don't be reactionary:** Let things run their course. When things happen, educate the kids on how to handle them.
+ **Do nothing:** Essentially do little business transition planning. Yes, the wills may be complete and the estate planning taken care of, but not much else in the business has been addressed.
  > What more needs to be said? Well, there are a few things. Why is it that death seems to be the one thing that everyone runs from? I won't answer that here as many books have been written on this topic. The more we plan for the eventual result of life, the more we can relax and enjoy ourselves. Stop playing God and being afraid of death. Know that death will come and your job—yes, your JOB—is to make sure the next generation is adequately prepared. That means helping them learn how to make decisions. Let them disagree with you; provide them your counsel, but let them make the decisions. Let them learn how to fall, pick themselves up again and fall. Read John Maxwell's *Failing Forward*; it will change your perspective. If they can't run the business while you are around, why do you believe they will do a better job when you are dead?

Financials are often a great way to pull in an outsider to help with the leadership of the organization. Unfortunately, this creates fear in many small business owners stemming from the lack of control it creates and the fear of being ripped off, stolen from, swindled and otherwise taken advantage of. There is a difference between delegation and abdication. Most of the negative stories you hear are truly from abdication and not

COACH'S CORNER

Passion

These recommendations can vary greatly depending on the role you are looking to get leadership from. If the business lacks vision from the owners, then one opportunity might be to consider selling some or all of the ownership. This does not come without introspection and hopefully coaching. All business owners go through periods of lost focus, drudgery and exhaustion. How long this lasts depends on the next step. If you enjoy the product side of the business and dislike the business operations, then hire someone to handle operations. It is not a failure to have someone else run your business. In fact, I would contend it is the greatest level of success to recognize what you want and do it.

delegation. You cannot hire someone, give them the keys to the vault and then wonder why they ripped you off. There are countless checks and balances that can be put in place to ensure quality without risk. Most CPAs can provide you checklists for these types of check and balances. They include:

- Give different people the responsibility for writing checks and doing the bank reconciliations.
- Have standard key performance indicators (KPIs) that are measured month to month and year to year.
- Delegate but don't abdicate—which means give them responsibilities, but validate the work and information on a regular basis
- Know your numbers. Review your financial statements monthly, for example.
  - › Revenue
  - › Profit margin
  - › Gross margin

> Revenue / Expense ratio
> Days sales outstanding
> Return on investment
> Cash in bank
> Cost of goods sold
> Inventory turns per year
> Cash flow
> Return on capital
> Bank overdraft
> Inventory
> Aged accounts receivable
> Aged accounts payable
> Sales per square foot
> EBITDA
> Capital expenditure
> Debt to equity ratio
> R&D expenditure
> Training expenditure
> Marketing expenditure
> Depreciation
> Fixed assets
> Current liabilities
> Interest expenses
> Bad debts
> Discounts given/taken

Often no one can sell the product or service like the owner. The owner has that passion, knowledge and a "the buck stops here" mentality. That is fine; then be the salesperson, enjoy it and reap the results. However, if the concept of you being a salesperson brings only negative thoughts, then consider bringing in someone to take that burden. This is probably the hardest spot to fill in a family-owned business—or any business for that matter. Good salespeople are truly hard to find, are expensive and are temperamental. At their core, they are hard to manage, occasionally moody and can act the prima donna. Yet good ones are worth their weight in gold. I would venture to say that hiring a good salesperson often takes more than one attempt. I highly recommend giving behavioral assessments and sales tests to see if they can sell as well as they say they can. Do they truly have what it takes? Long and short, sales are the lifeblood of the business, so don't cut corners in this area.

Hire from outside the family if you need to. However, understand that they aren't family and they can and will move on at some point. That is not necessarily bad, so don't take it as a personal affront when they do. A good outsider will provide perspective, expertise and the ability for you to either grow or do the things you enjoy. This also ties to the ability to allow for opportunity to progress within the company, which is critical to longer term success. Don't fear it; embrace the concept—when done right you will not regret it.

CHAPTER 16

Creating the Legacy

Your legacy is what you want it to be. You can leave your legacy through you reputation or service, your name on a park bench or building, or your children and grandchildren. You are the only one who can create your legacy. The legacy of your business is also at your discretion. Not considering what your legacy will be will generate mediocrity. But note that not everyone has to be remembered for solving the world's problems.

The paint store back in New England was a wonderful place to go. Smitty and Kathy ran the store for many, many years. Their son worked with them as well, serving the customers and making sure the store operated smoothly (and probably to give Mom and Dad some time off). Smitty was a wonderful husband and business owner. He didn't have all the latest gadgets, but he knew his business. He took care of his customers. He built relationships. He educated his customers on how to paint and what type of paint was needed. He knew who your spouse was, what type of wallpaper you put up five years ago and the color of the trim. To this day, when I think of paint I think back to what Smitty taught me.

Smitty left a legacy to me and to many others back in that New England town. Smitty may not even be alive today. He sold his business, and he and his wife retired. The new place just wasn't the same, however. The new owners updated things and made it "more customer friendly," but they really didn't. We stopped going there and went to a big-box store instead. Once the relationship was gone, our focus was price. Smitty had taught me how to buy paint and how to care about customers. That was his legacy.

For some the legacy will be about passing the business to the next generation; for others the legacy will be financial security. Some will see their legacy in the products they manufactured, the safety they provided to families and how they served their customers.

> *Smitty had taught me how to buy paint and how to care about customers. That was his legacy.*

Smitty really provided a number of legacies. Aside from the legacy he left his customers was the financial foundation he provided for his children and grandchildren. Let's be realistic: The family business is about the business and making money. If we aren't looking to make money, then why are we working all those long hours, taking the risks and trying to create an environment for the future of the family?

One of the newsletters I read on a regular basis talks about the lack of value creation in today's entrepreneurial environment. Family businesses are entrepreneurial at heart. Yet as long as they are only looking to pay today's bills, they aren't creating value. Does that sound harsh? Yes, it is, but that's intentional. Survival is not a legacy, not good for the business and not good for the community. Creating value that can be built upon, can be sold and can generate revenue and. more importantly, profit is absolutely critical not only for your family but also for the community. A business that just scrapes by doesn't contribute to a community that grows, thrives and entices others to try starting a business. The business isn't providing value back into the community—they are merely surviving.

You wonder why your kids don't want to go into the business. Why should they? You worked long hours, paid yourself little and then couldn't retire with any level of comfort. Is that the legacy you are trying to leave? Leaving a legacy takes planning and requires risk but also generates value.

Your Business Legacy

Do you want your business to continue after you are no longer running it—Should you pass it to the next generation or sell it to non-family buyers—you need to have built a legacy of value, profits and customers who return or refer you to others. Ask yourself the following questions about your business to see if you are leaving a good legacy:

+ If you were going to buy a business, would you want the business to revolve around the owners? In other words, if the owners were to walk away from the business, no one else knows enough about the business to keep it operating. Too many family-operated businesses are so intertwined with the family that if the family were not present, there would not be a business.
+ Has the business generated profits year after year? If not, why would someone else purchase it?
+ Is the business so leveraged with debt that even if you could sell it, there would not be anything else left of value?
+ What is the future of the product you are selling or the service you are providing? Are you essentially in the horse and buggy business, one with no future or that is a shadow of what it was?
+ Are you reinventing yourselves on a regular basis, trying new things and looking at the business through the perspective of your customers or your vendors?

Another perspective of legacy is determining what you want this family business to look like. So often the business essentially looks like a patchwork quilt, made up of leftover pieces all thrown together. Someone with an artistic touch can make a masterpiece out of it, yet the masterpiece is only created through a great deal of planning.

COACH'S CORNER
What's Your Legacy?

- Create an organization chart of what the business needs to look like three years from now. Who cares if the same name is in many of the spots in the organization chart? Doing this exercise begins to provide a vision of what the business can grow to be. Who is the controller, the marketing manager, the salesperson? Who is the president, the product quality manager? And so on. What do you want the company to look like? If you dream and lay out the plan, you have a far greater chance of making that plan a reality.

- Consider your legacy. Sometimes a legacy can be woven into a mission and vision statement for the business. You will have a legacy upon death. You have a choice now as to what it will be. Do you want control of it or do you want it to just happen?

- Intentionally create a business that will work without you and your family. You, your business and your family will be forever grateful.

- Profit, profit, profit. Have a plan to generate profits each and every year. Don't pay yourself what is left over. Pay yourself and also generate a profit. You can sell an unprofitable business but not for as much as a profitable one. The choice is yours.

But doesn't everyone know how to do these things? Actually no, not everyone knows how to sell, market, read financial statements, be a visionary, and so on. Yet, now is the time to start passing the reins of the business to the next generation. What do they know about all the aspects of the business? Are you as the owner teaching that next generation? Are you open to them doing things in new and different ways?

One of my clients had a fantastic business. They served the community well and they knew how to deliver great customer service. They had survived and thrived for more than 30 years in the business. It was time to start handing over the reins of the business to the children, four of them in total. Yet which ones knew how to negotiate with bankers, read financial statements, make buying decisions and be the visionary that leads to the next generation? Some of that is not taught; it is a gift and it is learned through years of trial and error. Teach your next generation how to determine margins, read financial statements, how to determine if the risk is one worth taking. This is not an overnight learning process. You didn't learn it in a short period of time, so why would they? And when you learned, the business was smaller, times were different and risk may be even greater now. Therefore, the next generation must know and understand how the business is run—especially financials. Financials for most families is the big black hole that few understand unless they have the benefit of an accounting background.

Start early and start sharing. Help everyone understand the impact of market share, profitability, discounts, pricing, cost of goods sold, overhead and the list goes on. Take on one topic per month and you will soon have a new generation of very knowledgeable family members who can make decisions quickly enough to make a difference.

CHAPTER 17

Passing the Torch

Mom and Dad are now in their 70s. They are still active in the business, yet the reality is they need to be stepping back and delegating more control and decisions to the three children in the business. The three kids have been a part of the business for multiple years so they know how it works and how to provide the service and deliver the product. Sounds like a great scenario, right? Well, that depends.

So often the product and service areas are running smoothly, yet the next generation doesn't have a great grasp of the business portion.

Financials. How do you read those financials? Why is the overhead rate so important and how does that relate to cost of goods sold and profitability? Who is our banker and why is that relationship so important? How does the profitability trend? If seasonal, what is it per season? Business is math, marketing is math, team is math, sales is math, so why wouldn't financials be math? If you don't like math, then find someone who does and can translate it to what you can understand. As the transition begins, understanding the numbers becomes more critical than anything else. High profitability can cover up many sins, but good math can weed them out and increase profitability even more.

- ◆ Management of the team. How does Mom stimulate, encourage and manage the team? Will the team be ready, willing and able to work for the next generation? Does the next generation have the leadership skills in place to be wise beyond their years? It takes five components to ensure you have the team you want:
  - › Leadership strength
  - › SMART goals for the entire team (**S**pecific, **M**easurable, **A**chievable, **R**esults driven and **T**ime based)
  - › Consistent rules that everyone lives by and can grow by
  - › Right attitude
  - › Support for risk taking
- ◆ Vision. Who will now carry the vision for the business? Who will take the trends affecting the business and start to make plans now to make the necessary course adjustments? Who balances the visionary to keep a level of reality in place? One business I worked with had an environment where the husband was the visionary. He always had new ideas, new thoughts, new opportunities that he wanted to follow. The wife was more of the money manager and brought a dose of reality to the business. She is the one who asked the hard questions regarding return on investment, the downside to an idea, etc. That is a valuable role to have in any company. However, that must be moderated with the vision that sometimes can't be seen by anyone else. Too much caution allows opportunities to pass and therefore be missed.

My parents had one such opportunity. Dad was offered the opportunity to get in on the ground floor of a development that was taking place in the area where they lived. At the time, the area was essentially in the middle of nowhere. Actually it was in between somewhere big and somewhere else that was growing. The place in between was a risk. The cows that lived in that field were pretty content. Now today that area is a bustling, vibrant area. Dad always said that was the one that got away. This isn't to blame Mom; she always provided that caution, yet usually went with the visionary.

The next generation needs to have the visionary *and* the realist. There must be compromise between the two. One without the other can run the business into the ground. The visionary without the realist who asks the hard questions creates a business that follows every new trend. Not all trends are good. The realist is usually so cautious that they never get on the upswing of the bell curve. They are the late adopters and implement something after it is mainstream, passing up the opportunity to gain a competitive edge. It is sort of like installing a fax machine in 1995 when email was becoming the predominant tool. The fax machine was leading-edge back in the 1970s and was going out of style by the time the 90s rolled around.

> *Business is math, marketing is math, team is math, sales is math, so why wouldn't financials be math?*

- New blood. This becomes one of the greatest challenges for family business owners. As the company grows, employees need to be part of the future of the company. Yet what growth is available to non-family members? Unless you have a really huge family that all want to work in the company, there will need to be non-family members. Assuming you are hiring good, qualified team members, they don't want to be in the same position doing the same thing in five or 10 years. They want growth and opportunity. Is there potential for growth in your business? If there isn't, then make sure that is clear upon hiring; otherwise, continual hiring and replacing employee's impacts profitability and the running of the business.

It is your choice if you want a career path for employees. That is the joy of being the business owner. If you don't, then measure the impact of not being able to hire the best for the business. The best will always want to grow. Those who want to be in the same place probably won't last anyway. It is your choice, but understand the cost of your decision.

The best advice I heard from the owners of a family business on this topic was: Don't hire people unless you know their desires to advance. There are many people who want a job and that is it. They can be long-term employees who you can build a wonderful business with without the challenge of creating an advancement path.

Business Founders

There is a well known concept in the entrepreneurial community that the founders of the business must often step aside for the business to flourish. Dealing with founders is often very difficult. The business is their child, they have watched it grow up and flourish. They have pushed it through the teenage years of business growth. Now the business can really take off. Yet the founder is often not the one to capitalize on that growth. It is time to sell, turn over the reins and back away.

This is why many business acquisitions allow the founder to be around during a transistion but often not long term. The new owners need and want to make changes and the founder stands in the way. This conept is also true for the family business. Sometimes the best thing for the business is for the family to sell and back away. The next phase of growth may best happen through someone else, another family or another corporate environment. It is still part of your legacy of what you accomplished.

The challenge is to not hold on past your time. The challenge is to know when is that time. Not all business owners can take a business to the next level. It may not be their desire, passion or skill set. Acceptance is critical. Letting go is mandatory. Without acceptance and letting go you could create the end of the business. Your strong advisory team that was outlined earlier in the book can help you see the best path, outline the direction and help achieve the transition which is best for everyone.

Making a Smooth Transition

The transition from one generation to another can be very seamless and smooth. That takes education, planning, openness and humility.

- **Education.** Learning the business requires its own education process. That education is often not found in the halls of schools, but in the halls of the business, working with customers, walking hand in hand with employees. Learning what it means to make payroll, pay taxes, the impacts of discounting and generating new revenue. This education is the foundation of value for transitioning to a new generation. The education involves the next generation proving themselves, showing vision, seizing opportunities and learning the business from top to bottom. It involves at a minimum a season. What a season is—depends on the business. Seasons for business can span multiple years. Economic seasons can be 7 to 10 year cycles (winter—harsh economic conditions, spring—times of new growth opportunities, summer—high growth, fall retrenching of the business and the direction it is heading. The season will allow a full level of education which can be the difference between success and failure of the future business.

- **Planning.** The best way to ensure a smooth transition is to make a detailed plan. Talk about everything. Yes, I mean everything. I know—someone won't want to deal with the touchy subjects. Talk about them anyway. Create a plan that allows you to roll out of the company. Here is the reality: One of these days you will leave the company. It might be tomorrow, a year from now or a decade from now. It still doesn't change reality. Don't leave your next generation a mess and have them not know what to do. Make your business legacy live on—and not live on in chaos. If you want help in how to do that planning, call your team of advisors. The next generation will love you for it.

- **Openness.** Be willing to accept new ways of doing business, new products, new management style. Not all new is good, yet not all old is perfect. The next generation of leadership must make their own mistakes, but be there to guide them and keep them from falling off the cliff.

As much as possible, do away with the prejudices you have of this next generation about what they can and cannot do. Get rid of family politics. Stop protecting Junior and doing things for him. Let Junior stand on his own two feet or leave the business. There is no shame in not being in the family business. Life is too short to not follow your passion. A message to Junior: Understand that you will change. You may not want to join the business now, but your passions, needs, desires and interests will change as you age. Mom and Dad, Grandpa, my Aunt may start getting smarter and have a better perspective as you get out in the world, work a job and learn the realities of live. Don't burn your bridges and be unable/unwilling to come back and see the value of that family business. Also, following your passion doesn't mean sitting on the beach strumming a guitar (nothing against beaches and guitars). It does mean that if you have a passion for medicine and the family business is a furniture store, follow that passion for medicine. Just because your passion was the business doesn't mean you have to force your passion on everyone else.

- **Humility.** If someone lacks humility, have them start a business. If they still lack humility after running a business, try acquiring one or transitioning to another generation of leadership. It takes patience and the art of learning how to step back and let others accomplish the tasks in new ways. The second-generation owners of a family business whom I interviewed told the story of their dad. He had started to transition out of the business. He was very organized and had a place for everything. The son, the new business owner and leader, had not inherited that gift of organization. He had piles on his desk and on the table. Dad on a few occasions during the transition went through and "cleaned up" the piles and threw out what he believed was unnecessary papers. As you can imagine, that created tension and frustration—on both sides. New rules had to be set up. There were new ways of doing things. It wasn't better—just different—and Dad had to step back. He needed to be humble, understand new ways and allow the new regime to succeed or make mistakes on their own. Dad was no longer in control.

Timing the Transition

Transition timing can be very stressful. How long will it take to transition parents out of the business? It seldom happens overnight (unless by death or divorce). Yet the multi-year transition can be enough to kill the business, the relationships or both. The challenges include:

- Customers. Do customers always want to work with Dad, since he gives them a long-term customer discount that Junior won't? Do they like the way Mom runs the business and always ask for her, making it hard to establish a level of leadership?
- Boundaries. So who really is in charge? Daughter? Mom? Dad? All of the above? Who makes the decisions during the transition time? Create a plan that lays out the transition. Is this a six-month, 12-month or two-year plan? You may have to revise the plan at some point. Do not just go with the flow. It might work out, but there is a great chance that it might not. Hoping things will go well doesn't work. Hoping no one will get their feelings hurt doesn't happen. Not making a plan puts you on a path to having issues.
- "But we have always done it this way." That statement has been heard around the world in businesses of all sizes. Family business owners do not have the corner on this market. It does take on a

new twist when changes need to take place to keep up with the times, the skills of the next generation or just market changes. One of my favorite books is *If It Ain't Broke, Break It* by Robert Kriegel and Louis Patler. Their concept is to examine conventional business wisdom and to break those rules in order to gain a competitive advantage. This book was written in the '90s but much of it still applies today. When something is working, you need to analyze why it is working and what can be done to improve how it is working. In other words, what can be done to make things work better? Football for many years was solely a running game. Even after the forward pass was legalized, it remained a running game until a coach decided to have his team try throwing the ball. Everyone was shocked and critical. Yet, today football is very much a throwing game; just look at what quarterbacks get paid for their throwing ability

> › Specific roles. Who does what needs to be specific, not general. Develop that organization chart. Who performs each of the roles in your company? Accounting, visioning, sales, customer management, collections, finances (which is probably different from accounting) and the list goes on. The clearer the roles, the less conflict and there is less chance that items fall through the cracks.

Conclusion

Family businesses are wonderful and the backbone of the world. Done correctly, they can be wonderful. Done poorly, they can be devastating. It is your choice regarding the advice, input, recommendations or suggestions you choose to follow. Know, however, that the choice is yours and you will reap the rewards of your decisions.

COACH'S CORNER

Summary

In case you looked to the end of the book and only want to read one page!

+ Plan, plan, plan.
+ Communicate with the family regularly.
+ Don't stick your head in the sand and ignore problems.
+ Create boundaries for work and family
+ Get advisors from outside the family.
+ Never stop learning and reading.
+ Make money so you can take more vacations, give to others, laugh more and enjoy your family since they are a gift to you each and every day.

Books to Read

General

Rich Dad, Poor Dad
  Robert Kiyosaki

Think and Grow Rich
  Napoleon Hill

How to Win Friends and Influence People
  Dale Carnegie

Start with Why: How Great Leaders Inspire Everyone to Take Action
  Simon Sinek

Mastering The Rockefeller Habits
  Verne Harnish

The Upside of Fear
  Weldon Long

Up, Down or Sideways: How to Succeed When Times Are Good, Bad or In Between
  Mark Sanborn

Finance

Accounting Made Simple
  Mike Piper

Sales

Action Selling: How to Sell Like a Professional, Even If You Think You Are One
Duane Sparks

The Accidental Salesperson
Chris Lytle

The Little Red Book of Selling
Jeffrey Gitomer (and all of Jeffrey Gitomer's books)

Customer Service

Uncommon Service
Frances Frei and Anne Morriss

Purple Cow: Transform Your Business by Being Remarkable
Seth Godin

Raving Fans: A Revolutionary Approach to Customer Service
Ken Blanchard and Sheldon Bowles

What Clients Love
Harry Beckwith

Emotional Intelligence

Emotional Intelligence 2.0
Travis Bradberry and Jean Greaves

Emotional Intelligence: Why It Can Matter More Than IQ
Daniel Goleman

StrengthsFinder 2.0
Tom Rath

Communication

Who do You Think You Are Anyway?
Robert A Rohm, PhD. and E. Chris Carey

The Question Before the Question:
John G. Miller

Conflict Resolution and Failure

Getting to Yes: Negotiating Agreement Without Giving In
Roger Fisher, William L. Ury, and Bruce Patton

Failing Forward
John Maxwell

Team

The No Asshole Rule: Building a Civilized Workplace and Surviving One That Isn't
Robert I. Sutton

The Five Dysfunctions of a Team
Patrick Lencioni

The Advantage: Why Organizational Health Trumps Everything Else in Business
Patrick Lencioni

Leadership

The 21 Irrefutable Laws of Leadership
John Maxwell

The 15 Invaluable Laws of Growth
John Maxwell

What Got You Here Won't Get You There
Marshall Goldsmith

Management

Multipliers: How the Best Leaders Make Everyone Smarter
Liz Wiseman

Outliers:
Malcom Gladwell

Company Culture

Delivering Happiness: A Path to Profits, Passion, and Purpose
Tony Hsieh

The Starbucks Experience: 5 Principles for Turning Ordinary into Extraordinary
Joseph A. Michelli

Good to Great
Jim Collins

Great Choice
Jim Collins and Morten T. Hansen

Nuts! Southwest Airline's Crazy Recipe for Business and Personal Success
Kevin and Jackie Freiberg

Time Management

The Seven Habits of Highly Effective People
Stephen R. Covey

Making It All Work
David Allen

Time Traps: Proven Strategies for Swamped Salespeople
Todd Duncan

Be Excellent at Anything
Tony Schwartz

First Things First
Stephen R. Covey, A. Roger Merrill and Rebecca R. Merrill

The Myth of Multitasking
David Crenshaw

Getting Things Done
David Allen

JANNA HOIBERG

ACTION COACH · LEADERSHIP · DESIRE · VISION · DETERMINATION

Why Choose Me to Speak at Your Next Event?

"I understand the business world through real life experience. I work hard at being congruent to what I teach. One of my differentiators is my 30 plus years of experience in managing and operating successful small Businesses. And I'm still studying, researching and applying what I learn about running businesses today, both with my clients and in the community. I guarantee you will enjoy, learn, be challenged and be able to apply what you learn from the event."

—JANNA HOIBERG, Executive and Leadership Business Coach

As an Executive and Leadership Business Coach, Janna has had the opportunity to help businesses from start-up ventures through large organizations increase their profits, improve their systems, strengthen team and executive leadership, and grow their companies significantly. Janna has been successful because of her vast array of Executive and Leadership positions in various organizations, offering an abundance of Marketing, Operations, and Sales experience to her clients.

Janna will become your marketing manager, your sales director, your training coordinator, your confidant, and your mentor. She will help you make your dreams come true. The diversity of Janna's background will be a valuable asset as she helps you overcome the challenges that both you and your business face.

To contact Janna, please:
CALL: (719) 358-6936,
EMAIL: janna@jannahoiberg.com
or send an information request by using
the online contact forms at
http://www.jannahoiberg.com